New Directions for
Child and Adolescent
Development

Lene Arnett Jensen
Reed W. Larson
EDITORS-IN-CHIEF

William Damon
FOUNDING EDITOR

Exemplar Methods and Research: Strategies for Investigation

M. Kyle Matsuba
Pamela Ebstyne King
Kendall Cotton Bronk
EDITORS

Number 142 • Winter 2013
Jossey-Bass
San Francisco

EXEMPLAR METHODS AND RESEARCH: STRATEGIES FOR INVESTIGATION
M. Kyle Matsuba, Pamela Ebstyne King, Kendall Cotton Bronk (eds.)
New Directions for Child and Adolescent Development, no. 142
Lene Arnett Jensen, Reed W. Larson, Editors-in-Chief

Microfilm copies of issues and articles are available in 16 mm and 35 mm, as well as microfiche in 105 mm, through University Microfilms, Inc., 300 North Zeeb Road, Ann Arbor, Michigan 48106-1346.

ISSN 1520-3247   electronic ISSN 1534-8687

NEW DIRECTIONS FOR CHILD AND ADOLESCENT DEVELOPMENT is part of The Jossey-Bass Education Series and is published quarterly by Wiley Subscription Services, Inc., a Wiley company, at Jossey-Bass, One Montgomery Street, Suite 1200, San Francisco, CA 94104-4594. Postmaster: Send address changes to New Directions for Child and Adolescent Development, Jossey-Bass, One Montgomery Street, Suite 1200, San Francisco, CA 94104-4594.

New Directions for Child and Adolescent Development is indexed in Cambridge Scientific Abstracts (CSA/CIG), CHID: Combined Health Information Database (NIH), Contents Pages in Education (T&F), Educational Research Abstracts Online (T&F), Embase (Elsevier), ERIC Database (Education Resources Information Center), Index Medicus/MEDLINE (NLM), Linguistics & Language Behavior Abstracts (CSA/CIG), Psychological Abstracts/PsycINFO (APA), Social Services Abstracts (CSA/CIG), SocINDEX (EBSCO), and Sociological Abstracts (CSA/CIG).

INDIVIDUAL SUBSCRIPTION RATE (in USD): $89 per year US/Can/Mex, $113 rest of world; institutional subscription rate: $388 US, $428 Can/Mex, $462 rest of world. Single copy rate: $29. Electronic only–all regions: $89 individual, $388 institutional; Print & Electronic–US: $98 individual, $450 institutional; Print & Electronic–Canada/Mexico: $98 individual, $490 institutional; Print & Electronic–Rest of World: $122 individual, $524 institutional.

EDITORIAL CORRESPONDENCE should be e-mailed to the editors-in-chief: Lene Arnett Jensen (ljensen@clarku.edu) and Reed W. Larson (larsonr@illinois.edu).

Jossey-Bass Web address: www.josseybass.com

CONTENTS

Bronk, K. C., King, P. E., & Matsuba, M. K. (2013). An introduction to exemplar research: A definition, rationale, and conceptual issues. In M. K. Matsuba, P. E. King, & K. C. Bronk (Eds.), *Exemplar methods and research: Strategies for investigation. New Directions for Child and Adolescent Development, 142,* 1–12.

1

An Introduction to Exemplar Research: A Definition, Rationale, and Conceptual Issues

Kendall Cotton Bronk, Pamela Ebstyne King, M. Kyle Matsuba

Abstract

The exemplar methodology represents a useful yet underutilized approach to studying developmental constructs. It features an approach to research whereby individuals, entities, or programs that exemplify the construct of interest in a particularly intense or highly developed manner compose the study sample. Accordingly, it reveals what the upper ends of development look like in practice. Utilizing the exemplar methodology allows researchers to glimpse not only what is but also what is possible with regard to the development of a particular characteristic. The present chapter includes a definition of the exemplar methodology, a discussion of some of key conceptual issues to consider when employing it in empirical studies, and a brief overview of the other chapters featured in this volume. © 2013 Wiley Periodicals, Inc.

NEW DIRECTIONS FOR CHILD AND ADOLESCENT DEVELOPMENT, no. 142, Winter 2013 © Wiley Periodicals, Inc.
Published online in Wiley Online Library (wileyonlinelibrary.com). • DOI: 10.1002/cad.20045

Although exemplar research and methods have been more prominent in the last two decades within the developmental sciences (i.e.,
Bronk, 2008; Colby & Damon, 1992; Frimer & Walker, 2009; Hart
& Matsuba, 2009; Reimer, Goudelock, & Walker, 2009), the strategy of using expert participants in research emerged early in the 20th century (see
Allport, 1942; Murray, 1938). Such methods have been used effectively to
explore lesser-understood and multifaceted domains of development by engaging the exemplar-participant as a collaborator in investigation. This volume seeks to introduce exemplar research to a wider audience. As a means
of introduction, this chapter includes a definition of the methodology, an
explanation of why it is important, and a discussion of some of the key
conceptual issues to consider when applying it.

Definition and Use

The exemplar methodology has been around since Aristotle's time. While
Aristotle did not conduct empirical studies, he was interested in, among
other things, the study of ethics. He believed that ethics was a practical
rather than a theoretical matter, and as such, to learn about the development
of ethics, virtues, and character, he examined highly ethical, virtuous, and
wise individuals. In *Nicomachean Ethics* he wrote, "We approach the subject
of practical wisdom by studying the persons to whom we attribute it" (trans.
1962, 6.5 1140a25). In other words, to understand how a complex construct
functions and develops, it made sense to examine that construct in the lives
of individuals who exhibited it in an intense and highly developed manner.

Maslow (1971) was one of the earliest scholars to actually employ an
exemplar methodology in a research context. Interested in understanding
how people achieve self-actualization, Maslow focused his research on individuals he believed were fully self-actualized. Development, he claimed, "is
learning to grow and learning what to grow toward" (p. 169). Like Aristotle,
Maslow argued that if we want to learn about ultimate human potential, we
should study highly functional and enlightened individuals. The exemplar
methodology represents an approach to research based on this philosophy.

More specifically, the exemplar methodology is a sample selection technique that involves the intentional selection of individuals, groups, or entities that exemplify the construct of interest in a particularly intense or
highly developed manner (Bronk, 2012b). In using the exemplar methodology, researchers deliberately identify and study a sample of individuals
or entities that exhibit a particular characteristic in an exceptional manner. In this way, the exemplar methodology features participants who are
rare, not from the perspective of the characteristics they exhibit, but in
the highly developed manner with which they demonstrate those particular
attributes.

The primary strength of exemplar research is its ability to reveal what
the leading edge of development entails. Exemplars reveal what complete or

nearly complete development looks like in real life. Whenever more typical individuals become capable of exhibiting actions indicative of the construct of interest, they are tracing the steps of where the exemplars have already been (Damon & Colby, this volume).

However, exemplars are not necessarily far removed from more typical individuals. For instance, they exhibit the same characteristics as others, only in a more highly developed manner. Further, while their development is exemplary in at least one area, it is likely to be typical or even deficient in other areas. For example, moral exemplars exhibit highly developed commitments to moral aims, but they do not necessarily have particularly highly developed social or cognitive abilities.

Because exemplars are similar to typical individuals in other regards, what we learn from them can be applied to people who demonstrate less complete but more common development around the construct of interest. In other words, what we learn from the exemplars can illuminate more typical developmental processes. Colby and Damon (1992), in writing about moral exemplars, note that "Great moral acts . . . spring from the same source as lesser ones" (p. 4). Put another way, moral exemplars are likely to perform more consequential moral acts than typical individuals, but they do so in essentially the same way.

Use of the exemplar methodology has increased in conjunction with the growth of the positive psychology movement (Benson & Scales, 2009; Damon, 2004; Seligman & Csikszentmihalyi, 2000; Sheldon & King, 2001). Historically, psychologists have been concerned with understanding what can go wrong with regard to human behavior, emotions, social interactions, and cognition. The focus of this one-sided field of human functioning has brought about a highly developed knowledge of people's mental vulnerabilities, deficiencies, and illnesses, but it has largely ignored issues of human thriving and flourishing (Bundick, Yeager, King, & Damon, 2010; Seligman, 2011; Wissing, 2000). Leaders in the field of psychology, recognizing the need for a deeper understanding of people's inner strengths and overall well-being, helped establish the new paradigm of positive psychology. As the number of studies based on this new paradigm has increased, so too has use of the exemplar methodology. The exemplar methodology lends itself to the study of optimal human development because of its focus on highly developed individuals. As a result, recent exemplar studies have tended to focus on "positive" constructs.

The exemplar methodology has been employed in qualitative, quantitative, and mixed-methods research designs. Historically, the exemplar methodology was used most commonly in qualitative studies situated within the broader case study tradition. Gordon Allport (1942), one of the early proponents of case study approaches, argued that idiographic methods were useful for countering the "thinness" of nomothetic methods.

In qualitative exemplar studies, researchers first design nomination criteria that will be used to qualify potential participants as exemplars.

Ideal nomination criteria are as concrete as possible, and at once narrow enough to be descriptive of a particularly highly developed group of individuals, but at the same time broad enough to capture a range of experiences and characteristics within the exemplary sample (Bronk, 2012b). In some cases, nomination criteria are generated by the researchers themselves (e.g., Damon, 2008), and in other cases, they are generated by relevant experts (e.g., Colby & Damon, 1992). The precise nature of the nomination criteria is determined by the nature of the study. For example, a study of young care exemplars used the following as its nomination criteria: Youth care exemplars are involved in community, church, or youth group activities that benefit others; they have unusual or admirable family responsibilities; they exhibit a willingness to help those in need; they volunteer their time to help others; they display emotional and social maturity; they lead others; they practice open-mindedness about others; they demonstrate a willingness to look beyond the difficulties of living in an urban locale to a better future; they show compassion; they display a sense of humility about themselves; and they demonstrate a commitment to friends and family (Hart & Fegley, 1995, p. 1350). A study of youth purpose exemplars used the following criteria: Youth purpose exemplars demonstrate an enduring commitment to a long-term aim; they report that the aim is central to who they are; they are actively involved in working toward that aim and have plans for continuing to do so in the future; and they are committed to that aim at least in part because it allows them to contribute to the world beyond themselves (Bronk, 2012a, pp. 83–84).

Once nomination criteria have been established, they are shared with nominators who use them to identify potential exemplars. Nominators typically include relevant experts. Accordingly, in a study of moral exemplars, nominators included moral philosophers, ethicists, theologians, historians, and social scientists (Colby & Damon, 1992), and in a study of spiritual exemplars, they included spiritual leaders and scholars from a wide range of religious and spiritual backgrounds (King, 2010). Researchers then select a sample from the pool of nominated exemplars that is typically balanced for age, gender, ethnicity, or other relevant demographic variables.

Often qualitative exemplar studies are longitudinal and follow individuals over the course of a particularly important developmental period (Bronk, 2008, 2011, 2012a; Damon, 2008). Other times interviews are conducted only once, but in these cases they typically last several hours and feature accounts of participants' developmental journeys (Colby & Damon, 1992; Hart & Fegley, 1995; Matsuba & Walker, 2005). In keeping with the Aristotelian tradition, many qualitative exemplar studies have focused on aspects of moral and ethical development. For example, recent qualitative exemplar studies have featured samples of purpose exemplars (Bronk, 2005, 2008, 2011, 2012a), moral exemplars (Colby & Damon, 1992; MacRenato, 1995; Mastain, 2007; Matsuba & Walker, 2005), spiritual exemplars (King, 2010), altruistic exemplars (Oliner & Oliner, 1988), bravery exemplars

(Walker & Frimer, 2007), and care exemplars (Hart & Fegley, 1995; Walker & Frimer, 2007).

There are many strengths of case study exemplar studies. First, they represent a person-centered approach to research. As such, they can provide a rich and textured view of the whole person and the entire construct. Because case study exemplar research avoids the granularity inherent in many other methodologies, it has been used with some regularity by developmental psychologists interested in seeing how individuals who demonstrate virtues, developmental assets, indicators of thriving, and other positive characteristics develop and change over time (see Bronk, 2008, 2011, 2012a; Colby & Damon, 1992; Hart & Fegley, 1995).

Next, case study exemplar research provides an opportunity to view the leading edge of development in a real-world context. Whereas other research approaches often try to strip away the potentially muddying influences of experience, context, and confounding variables, the case study exemplar approach does not. As a result of focusing on the lived experience, the exemplar methodology can provide insights into the processes and experiences of a particular phenomenon that likely could not be gained in any other way. What does it look like to lead a life of caring (Hart & Fegley, 1995)? How do individuals who have dedicated their lives to service develop a moral sense (Colby & Damon, 1992)? How do young environmental exemplars view their work in relation to their emerging sense of self (Pratt, 2011)? Case study exemplar research is immensely useful in answering these types of process-oriented and experience-oriented developmental questions in real-world settings.

While the exemplar methodology is more commonly used in qualitative studies, it has also been used in quantitative research. In these cases, nomination criteria are intentionally broader in scope to produce a larger sample of exemplars. In a recent quantitative exemplar study (Matsuba & Walker, 2004), researchers asked the executive directors of a variety of social organizations to nominate young adults within their groups who had demonstrated "extraordinary moral commitments." An interpretation of what constituted an "extraordinary moral commitment" was left up to the lay nominators. Because the research team sought to identify exemplars who reflected a "folk" conception of moral excellence, the decision to use fairly vague nomination criteria and to include lay individuals as nominators was an intentional one; the team was concerned that expert nominators and more prescriptive nomination criteria would reflect too narrow a conception of morality. Other studies have similarly employed a *folk psychology* approach. For instance, Walker and Pitts (1998) polled college students to identify a normative understanding of morality. In other quantitative exemplar studies, nomination criteria have been based on winning a particular award. For example, Walker and Frimer (2007) selected a sample of care and bravery exemplars from a pool of individuals who had won care and bravery awards given out by the Canadian government.

Quantitative exemplar studies similarly offer clear advantages. With larger sample sizes, researchers are able to make predictions about the frequency and prevalence of their findings with the possibility of generalizing their results more broadly. Nevertheless, gathering larger samples of exemplars can be challenging depending on how restrictive researchers are in their conceptions of exemplarity.

Finally, the exemplar methodology is particularly useful in mixed-methods approaches (e.g., Matsuba & Walker, 2004; Walker & Frimer, 2007). For example, in a three-pronged approach to the study of youth purpose, researchers at the Stanford Center on Adolescence conducted a nationwide survey of young people's purposes in life (Damon, 2008). Surveys administered to a national sample of youth revealed the forms and prevalence of purpose among American youth today. A subset of individuals, whose survey responses suggested they were either deficient or typical in their commitment to purpose, was invited to participate in interviews. Finally, a small sample of highly developed purpose exemplars participated in in-depth, case study–style interviews, and this line of inquiry provided key insights into what the leading edge of the development of purpose looks like in practice. Taken together, this mixed-methods approach sheds light on deficient, typical, and exemplary forms of purpose among youth today. Accordingly, researchers were able to glean critical insights into the full spectrum of purpose development.

Strengths of the Exemplar Methodology

Whether as a part of a qualitative, quantitative, or mixed-methods study, the exemplar methodology offers an effective means of exploring unfamiliar areas of development. The moral exemplar studies published in the 1990s (i.e., Colby & Damon, 1992; Hart & Fegley, 1995) challenged the field of moral development and Kohlberg's reigning stage theory of the day. These studies expanded the current understanding of morality and introduced the importance of moral identity and moral judgment. Conclusions from these studies began to illuminate the complexities of the moral life and of living with sustained moral commitments.

A key strength of exemplar studies is the way they include participants as collaborators, considering participants' perspectives in investigation and analysis. Participants' experiences, beliefs, values, and meanings represent seminal data. The exemplar methodology rests on the assumption that participants manifest the phenomenon under investigation in a highly developed manner and are therefore experts who can provide valid input through surveys, questionnaires, and interviews. A study of youth purpose exemplars generated interesting and important findings regarding the origins of purpose that would not have been possible without including participants as co-collaborators. In interviews with the youth, researchers and participants discovered that the young people's purposes sprang from opportunities they encountered to apply their personal skills and talents to address personally meaningful social needs (Bronk, 2012a).

The nominating procedures inherent in an exemplar methodology are also useful for operationalizing complex psychological constructs. The emergence of the study of positive psychology, positive youth development, and human thriving ushered in a focus on optimal development and positive outcomes in children, youth, and adults. Although this "new vision" for what children and youth can become is inspiring, defining and operationalizing positive constructs in contextually and developmentally appropriate ways represents a significant challenge. Many of these constructs are informed by philosophical, ethical, cultural, or religious traditions in which psychologists are not well trained. For instance, psychology as a discipline is not equipped to define what *ought to be moral*, or what *ought to constitute thriving*, or what it *ought to mean to have purpose*. However, the exemplar methodology sets out a useful process for operationalizing these complex constructs. Identifying and applying nomination criteria, with input from relevant and well-informed scholars and practitioners, allows cultural and contextual norms to influence the operationalization of these constructs and to inform the nature of exemplarity. For example, in a recent study on spiritual exemplars, the research team turned to specific monotheistic congregations to identify criteria for nominating exemplars within their own congregations (Reimer & Dueck, 2012). Muslim congregants designed the criteria for nominating Muslim exemplars, and members of a synagogue identified the criteria for nominating Jewish exemplars. The criteria were intentionally nonstandard across religious traditions, since what it meant to be a religious exemplar varied by faith tradition. King (2010) used a different approach to designing nomination criteria to identify adolescent spiritual exemplars from six different countries. She and her team used an iterative process that drew on the current psychological literature and incorporated the perspective of expert panels of diverse scholars and practitioners. The result was a set of culturally sensitive nomination criteria that selected for more general expressions of spirituality in a wide range of faiths.

Conceptual Issues in Applying the Exemplar Methodology

While the exemplar methodology has many strengths, certain conceptual issues need to be considered before effectively employing it. Included in this are a number of key decisions that must be made, including the decision to focus on ideal states rather than more typical ones, the decision regarding who will identify exemplars, and finally the decision of whether to use a comparison sample.

An overarching assumption behind studying exemplars is that we can learn from individuals who demonstrate a particular characteristic in a highly developed way. However, while we argue there is much to be learned by studying these individuals, this issue has been a source of some debate. In Susan Wolf's (1982) article "Moral Saints," the author philosophically questions whether moral perfection is something to which we ought to strive so as to improve our well-being. In her portrayals, moral sainthood, which is represented by people who place priority in living according to set moral principles, such as moral utilitarianism, is both unappealing and unrealistic. Rather, most researchers who study exemplarity adopt a more naturalistic perspective and believe that more typical individuals possess, to a degree, the same capacities and traits as exemplars, and that through their own character or with the aid of social support, they too can realistically attain the level of exemplarity (Flanagan, 1993). While achieving exemplarity may not always be desirable, attaining fuller development of a particular characteristic may be, and exemplar research can be used to identify individual differences and social support factors that foster further growth within a specified domain.

Another salient conceptual issue involves who defines and operationalizes the exemplar construct. That is, who defines who and what an exemplar is. Typically, this process involves a number of steps. As previously outlined, individuals design the nomination criteria; nominators apply the criteria to identify a pool of potential exemplars; and researchers select a sample from that pool to include in the study. Researchers typically determine who is involved in each of these three steps. Take, for example, Colby and Damon's (1992) study of moral exemplars. In this study, the researchers influenced the selection process by determining who would generate the criteria, who would apply it, and which individuals from the pool of potential exemplars would be included in their study. In the case of Matsuba and Walker (2004), the researchers had people from municipal social organizations nominate moral exemplars within their organizations, and then justify their nominations. Finally, Walker and Frimer (2007) selected bravery and care exemplars based on national awards given by the Canadian government. However, it is unclear which exact criteria were used and who applied the criteria in choosing the award recipients.

What these examples from the moral field demonstrate is that how one selects exemplars will invariably influence how exemplarity is conceptualized in the study. For example, by asking social organizations for nominations, Matsuba and Walker (2004) captured the beneficent-caring facet of morality. Walker and Frimer (2007) captured both the caring and brave-courageous facets. Further, other people besides the researcher contribute to the nomination process and thus influence how exemplarity is conceived. In Colby and Damon's (1992) study, nomination criteria were generated by individuals who were highly educated in ethical matters, whereas Matsuba and Walker (2004) relied on lay conceptions of morality. Each group of individuals provided its conceptual understanding of moral exemplarity, and so the kinds of people nominated reflected each group's understanding of the morality construct.

NEW DIRECTIONS FOR CHILD AND ADOLESCENT DEVELOPMENT • DOI: 10.1002/cad

Not only do researchers need to consider who is involved in the sample selection process, but they also need to consider what constitutes being "highly developed" in some area. Conceptually and methodologically, exemplars are different from more typical individuals on some domain dimension. But, what point on this dimension do people have to pass in order for them to fall within the exemplar category? In most exemplar studies this is not clearly defined. For studies that use a list of criteria, nominators tend to simply check "yes" or "no" with regard to whether potential participants meet each criterion. In other studies, individuals rely on their intuition to determine whether potential participants meet the criteria. Whatever the strategy, what typically is not discussed is the mental standard upon which nominators are comparing their nominee. Researchers using the exemplar methodology should strive to make this clear.

In addition, researchers interested in using the exemplar methodology need to consider whether it makes sense to include a "comparison" group. Methodologically, many studies have included a normative group of individuals against which to compare exemplars. These have been useful in illustrating whether exemplars do, in fact, differ on the domains of interest and on other dimensions of interest to the researcher. However, one confound that typically is not controlled is the "placebo effect." Typically, researchers reveal to the exemplar participants the fact that they have been nominated as exemplars. Such an effect may account for the significant differences between the two groups. Few studies have addressed this issue.

Finally, the studies on exemplarity in this volume focus on positive, prosocial domains. What has not been integrated into this body of work are exemplarity studies in less positive, less prosocial domains. For example, what does exemplarity look like in the domain of business, sports, politics, organized crime, sociopathy? Certainly, there have been studies looking at exemplars in each of these areas. However, no other domain of exemplar studies—at least to our knowledge—includes the variety of methodological strategies or discussions of relevant conceptual issues.

It is important for researchers to consider these practical and conceptual issues when conducting exemplar research. We raise them not because we can offer easy or consistent solutions to them, but because we believe any study will be more effective if researchers have first thoughtfully considered them. The best solution is likely to be determined on a case-by-case basis, influenced by the particular nature of the exemplar study being conducted.

The Current Volume

Other chapters included in the current volume explore some of these conceptual issues in greater detail, highlight particular strengths of the methodology, and address some of the approach's more significant limitations. The second chapter, by William Damon and Anne Colby, provides an important rationale for the necessity of exemplar research. The authors argue that the use of high-performing exemplars as participants allows for an investigation of a *complete* account of an area of human functioning. They point out that social science studies without exemplar subjects can only yield a picture of deficient and typical growth; exemplars are needed to provide a picture of complete or nearly complete development. The third chapter by Lawrence J. Walker reviews a program of research that has led to the identification of motivational factors associated with moral behaviors. Specifically, the work of Walker and his colleagues identify agentic and communal motivations as predictors of moral behaviors, and they propose that within moral exemplars it is this synergy between these two motivations that forms the moral core.

The next chapter considers spiritual exemplars. Chapter 4, by Pamela Ebstyne King, Ross A. Oakes Mueller, and James Furrow, highlights the potential strengths of exemplar studies in exploring both common and particular expressions of human development. The authors discuss how the method's focus on exemplarity allows for the exploration of cultural ideals that are often overlooked by current developmental methodologies. By examining some of the distinctions between cross-cultural, cultural, and indigenous psychologies, the authors explain how nomination procedures, data gathering, and data analysis allow for universal and culturally specific investigations.

The fifth chapter, by M. Kyle Matsuba and Michael W. Pratt, offers insight into the development of environmental activists. Specifically, this study of committed environmental exemplars illuminates the processes and pathways leading to positive environmental behaviors. The authors offer a review of a sample of activists' lives, focusing on early childhood and adolescent experiences that contribute to a developmental model and identify pathways to developing an environmental identity.

The final contribution, by Daniel A. Hart, Theresa Murzyn, and Lisa Archibald, offers a critical commentary on the previous chapters and on use of the method in general. In addition to highlighting strengths and weaknesses of the exemplar methodology, Hart and his colleagues draw important distinctions between exemplarity research and biographical and psychobiographical research. They offer insight into why interest in this approach has grown recently and discuss the inspirational quality of exemplar studies.

Not only are exemplar strategies being used in developmental psychology, but they are also being used in neuropsychology and are relevant to social science researchers working in a variety of domains. This unique approach is timely, allowing for in-depth exploration of multifaceted and less understood domains of development that take personal, contextual, and cultural complexities into consideration.

References

Allport, G. W. (1942). *The use of personal documents in psychological science.* New York, NY: Social Science Research Center.

Aristotle. (1962). *Nicomachean ethics* (M. Ostwald, Trans.). Indianapolis, IN: The Library of Liberal Arts.

Benson, P. L., & Scales, P. C. (2009). The definition and preliminary measurement of thriving in adolescence. *The Journal of Positive Psychology, 4,* 85–104.

Bronk, K. C. (2005). *Portraits of purpose: A study examining the ways purpose contributes to positive youth development* (Doctoral dissertation). Retrieved from *UMI ProQuest Digital Dissertations.* (AAT 3187267)

Bronk, K. C. (2008). Humility among purpose exemplars. *Journal of Research in Character Education, 6*(1), 35–51.

Bronk, K. C. (2011). Portraits of purpose: The role of purpose in identity formation. In J. M. Mariano (Ed.), *New Directions in Youth Development: No. 132. Support and instruction for youth purpose* (pp. 31–44). San Francisco, CA: Jossey-Bass.

Bronk, K. C. (2012a). A grounded theory of the development of youth purpose. *Journal of Adolescent Research, 27,* 78–109. doi:10.1177/0743558411412958

Bronk, K. C. (2012b). The exemplar methodology: An approach to studying the leading edge of development. *Psychology of Well-Being: Theory, Research and Practice, 2*(5). doi:10.1186/2211-1522-2-5

Bundick, M. J., Yeager, D. S., King, P. E., & Damon, W. (2010). Thriving across the lifespan. In R. M. Lerner, M. E. Lamb, A. M. Freund, & W. F. Overton (Eds.), *Handbook of life-span development, Vol. 1: Cognition, biology and methods* (pp. 882–923). Hoboken, NJ: Wiley.

Colby, A., & Damon, W. (1992). *Some do care: Contemporary lives of moral commitment.* New York, NY: Free Press.

Damon, W. (2004). What is positive youth development? *The ANNALS of the American Academy of Political and Social Science, 591,* 13–24.

Damon, W. (2008). *The path to purpose: How young people find their calling in life.* New York, NY: Free Press.

Flanagan, O. (1993). *Varieties of moral personality: Ethics and psychological realism.* Cambridge, MA: Harvard University Press.

Frimer, J. A., & Walker, L. J. (2009). Reconciling the self and morality: An empirical model of centrality development. *Developmental Psychology, 45*(4), 1669–1681.

Hart, D., & Fegley, S. (1995). Prosocial behavior and caring in adolescence: Relations to self-understanding and social judgment. *Child Development, 66,* 1346–1359.

Hart, D., & Matsuba, M. K. (2009). Urban neighborhoods as contexts for moral identity development. In D. Narvaez & D. K. Lapsley (Eds.), *Personality, identity, and characters: Explorations in moral psychology* (pp. 214–231). New York, NY: Cambridge University Press.

King, P. (2010, March). *Spiritual exemplars from around the world: An exploratory study of spiritual development among adolescents.* Paper presented at the biennial meeting of the Society for Research on Adolescence, Philadelphia, PA.

MacRenato, S. W. (1995). *Experiences of moral commitment: A phenomenological study.* San Diego, CA: University of San Diego.

Maslow, A. (1971). *The farther reaches of human nature.* New York, NY: Viking Press.

Mastain, L. (2007). *The lived experience of altruism as described by moral exemplars: A descriptive phenomenological study* (Doctoral dissertation). Retrieved from *Dissertation Abstracts International,* DAI-B 67/12. (AAT 3246550)

Matsuba, M. K., & Walker, L. (2004). Extraordinary moral commitment: Young adults involved in social organizations. *Journal of Personality, 72,* 413–436.

Matsuba, M. K., & Walker, L. (2005). Young adult moral exemplars: The making of self through stories. *Journal of Research on Adolescence, 15*(3), 275–297.

Murray, H. A. (1938). *Explorations in personality.* New York, NY: Oxford University Press.

Oliner, S. P., & Oliner, M. P. (1988). *The altruistic personality: Rescuers of Jews in Nazi Europe: What led ordinary men and women to risk their lives on behalf of others?* New York, NY: Free Press.

Pratt, M. (2011, March). *Environmental memories of youth and adults: Identity and exemplar status predict story recall and level of detail.* Paper presented at the biennial meeting of the Society for Research on Child Development, Montreal, Canada.

Reimer, K. S., & Dueck, A. C. (2012). *The saints of 405: Spiritual identities of nominated monotheist exemplars.* Unpublished manuscript, Psychology Department, Fresno Pacific University, Fresno, CA.

Reimer, K., Goudelock, B. M., & Walker, L. J. (2009). Developing conceptions of moral maturity: Traits and identity in adolescent personality. *Journal of Positive Psychology, 4,* 372–388.

Seligman, M. (2011). *Flourishing: A visionary new understanding of happiness and well-being.* New York, NY: Free Press.

Seligman, M., & Csikszentmihalyi, M. (2000). Positive psychology: An introduction. *American Psychologist, 55,* 5–14.

Sheldon, K. M., & King, L. A. (2001). Why positive psychology is necessary. *American Psychologist, 56,* 216–217.

Walker, L. J., & Frimer, J. A. (2007). Moral personality of brave and caring exemplars. *Journal of Personality and Social Psychology, 93*(5), 845–860.

Walker, L. J., & Pitts, R. C. (1998). Naturalistic conceptions of moral maturity. *Developmental Psychology, 34,* 403–419.

Wissing, M. P. (2000, May). *Wellness: Construct clarification and a framework for future research and practice.* Keynote address at the first South African Wellness Conference, Port Elizabeth.

Wolf, S. (1982). Moral saints. *Journal of Philosophy, 79*(8), 419–439.

KENDALL COTTON BRONK *is an associate professor of educational psychology at Ball State University.*

PAMELA EBSTYNE KING *is an associate professor of marital and family studies with the Thrive Center for Human Development in the School of Psychology at Fuller Theological Seminary, Pasadena, California.*

M. KYLE MATSUBA *is a psychology instructor at Kwantlen Polytechnic University in Vancouver, BC, Canada.*

2

Why a True Account of Human Development Requires Exemplar Research

William Damon, Anne Colby

Abstract

This chapter uses moral psychology to illustrate why exemplar methods are essential for building a valid, complete understanding of key domains of human development. Social psychological, economic, and biological-evolutionary paradigms for studying morality rely on samples drawn from the general population. This research reveals a bleak picture of morality, highlighting its irrational, self-interested, externally controlled aspects. If the subjects in these studies are confused, pliable, or profit-maximizing, these studies conclude that people in general are morally irrational and self-interested. In contrast, studies that investigate morally exceptional individuals reveal a more thoughtful, ideal-driven, self-reflective, creative version of moral functioning. Any account that neglects this high-functioning segment of the range is seriously misleading and cannot provide the basis for aspiration or education. © 2013 Wiley Periodicals, Inc.

New Directions for Child and Adolescent Development, no. 142, Winter 2013 © Wiley Periodicals, Inc.
Published online in Wiley Online Library (wileyonlinelibrary.com). • DOI: 10.1002/cad.20046

T he validity of any finding in the behavioral sciences hinges on how well the study's investigatory procedures represent the topic of interest—or, in the term that most students learn in graduate school, how well the central constructs are *operationalized*. If the ways that the main constructs under investigation have been operationalized are weak, or even vigorously contested, the study's findings and implications become seriously suspect. One well-known example is provided by studies of intelligence as they have evolved over the past century.

The concept of intelligence covers an enormous range of mental capacities, including logic and other types of reasoning, practical and theoretical knowledge, critical and creative thinking, aesthetic sensibilities, common sense, street smarts, and so on. For this reason, Piaget defined intelligence as the many diverse mental functions that promote adaptation (Piaget, 1970), and Howard Gardner coined the phrase "multiple intelligences" to capture this diversity (Gardner, 1983, 2006). Nevertheless, social scientists have made sweeping claims about the nature and roots of human intelligence based only on people's responses to one or another version of the IQ test. Many researchers have used IQ as a proxy for human mental capacity *in general*, actually referred to as "g"—for general—in some incarnations of the test. (Indeed, an oft-quoted tribute to the powerful role of operational definitions in science had it that intelligence *is* simply what an IQ test measures.) Still, although IQ testing has yielded highly replicable findings related to the particular skills that such tests examine, many critics have doubted that these findings capture the nature and sources of intelligence more broadly understood. These critics point out that people's responses to IQ tests do not come close to representing the range of mental abilities that have created humanity's scientific, civic, business, spiritual, and artistic achievements, sometimes through feats of soaring genius (Gardner, 2011).

One index of a well-operationalized study is proper measurement. Another index, equally important, is the sample of subjects that the study examines and explains. For example, no account of human intelligence would be complete without a look at people who have been endowed with genius, as rare and unrepresentative as such people may be, because higher order intellectual functioning is a very consequential phenomenon and may have qualitatively different characteristics than ordinary mental processes. For a sensible sample design, measurement and sample selection must be coordinated. If a study is to capture what is special about how genius works, it may need to rely on different instruments and procedures than those designed to capture the contours of routine mental processes. Thus a sample of high-performing *exemplars* and a specially designed *exemplar methodology* are both required for a complete view of human intelligence.

To generalize from the study of intelligence, we argue that a reason to include exemplar samples in any scientific examination is to provide a complete account that applies to the full variety of human functioning. But this is only one part of our justification for exemplar research; we will also make another, stronger claim: An exemplar approach is necessary for providing an *accurate, nondistorted* account of any psychological phenomenon under investigation. Next we advance this claim with reference to the phenomenon of human morality, the topic of our own research programs over the past four decades.

The Nature and Sources of Morality

Social psychology textbooks, which mainly cover experimental research conducted with normative samples, generally paint a bleak picture of morality. Now-classic studies from social psychology have documented people's tendencies to shirk moral responsibility, conform to immoral demands, and act in inhumane ways when placed in challenging or tempting situations. Hartshorne and May (1928) showed that children will cheat when given the chance; Latane and Darley (1969) showed that bystanders will ignore screams for help; Milgram (1974) showed that people will subject others to painful levels of electric shock when instructed by an authority figure in a white coat to do so; Zimbardo (2007) showed that college students will abuse fellow students when placed in charge of them; and so on, down a litany of ignoble responses to experimental conditions.

Adding to this disheartening portrait of moral behavior are recent findings that have been interpreted as showing that people have little or no control over their responses to social situations, since we are mostly driven by our preprogrammed biological impulses. Among the advocates of this biological determinism is Nobel laureate Daniel Kahneman, who cites evidence such as the far higher tendency of judges to grant parole right after they have had lunch (Kahneman, 2011). Underlining the biological determinism of this position, a *New York Times* review of Kahneman's thesis was entitled "The amygdala made me do it" (Atlas, 2012).

Another proponent of the view that "morality is grounded in our biology" is former Harvard professor Marc Hauser, whose widely-quoted book *Moral Minds* promoted the view that moral behavior is instinctual, nonconscious, and outside our control. Hauser claims that "we evolved a moral instinct . . . designed to generate rapid judgments about what is morally right or wrong based on an unconscious grammar of action" (Hauser, 2006, p. xvii). Hauser bases his claims on evidence from experiments in which subjects are asked to respond to hypothetical dilemmas such as a runaway trolley car that has lost its brakes while heading toward hikers on the tracks. If the conductor lets the train stay on its course, five hikers will be run down. But if, instead, he steers the train in another direction, it will run down only one hiker who happens to be walking on a side track. The choice is whether to actively steer the train so as to kill one person intentionally or to passively allow the train to kill five times that number. When confronted with this dilemma, subjects decide quickly which choice they prefer, and magnetic images of their neural processes while they make their choices reveal patterns of activity in areas of their brains identified with moral emotion. Of course, this is an unlikely situation that poorly matches the experiences of real people. Yet, findings from this experiment have been used to make broad claims about morality, asserting that the moral response is dictated by biological dispositions. This biological determinism relegates the roles of judgment, belief, faith, conscience, and other forms of reflection and conscious choice to what is known in psychology as "epiphenomena"—that is, meaningless exercises in after-the-fact rationalization that play no part in actually determining behavior.

Another method of study in this biological paradigm is to trigger feelings of disgust by asking subjects to think about abhorrent activities such as incest between a brother and a sister or sex with dead chickens. In these scenarios, the investigator tries to rule out any rational basis for moral objections, asking respondents to assume, for example, that the amorous siblings will use birth control, will experience no psychological ill effects, and will keep their activities private. When subjects nevertheless recoil from such thoughts, a response Haidt calls "moral dumbfounding," their reactions are taken as evidence that morality is ruled by unconscious inborn emotions rather than by principled choice. Psychologist Jonathan Haidt writes that evidence of widespread moral dumbfounding shows "the importance of inborn moral intuitions [and] the socially functional (rather than truth-seeking) nature of moral thinking" (Haidt, 2007, p. 998).

Experimental studies from the discipline of economics also have contributed to the view that human behavior is determined by forces beyond our moral control. In the economic view, individual choices are determined by implicit calculations of risk and gain and the maximization of "utilities," which represent various aspects of the individual's self-interest. Experimental studies of behavior in economic games do sometimes grant the existence of altruism and preferences for solutions that are seen as fair. But such concerns are understood to be anomalies that only minimally affect the overall picture of the human condition as a collection of self-interested actors pursuing their own preferences or utilities (Kolm & Ythier, 2006).

Each of these research paradigms—the social psychological, biological, and economic—relies on samples of subjects drawn from the general population. The investigators have not been particularly concerned with the nature of these samples, which are considered to be representative of all people. If subjects in these studies are confused about the morality of contrived and improbable situations, pliable in carrying out nefarious commands from authoritative investigators, or profit-maximizing in economic games played with strangers, the conclusion in each case is that *people* are morally irrational, blindly obedient to authority, and fundamentally self-interested.

But the normative data from such samples fail to tell the whole story of morality. Some people do better than that, and most people can learn to do better. For example, studies using highly educated samples show very low levels of what Haidt has called "moral dumbfounding." It is primarily the less-educated participants who say that disgusting actions are *morally* wrong even if they cause no harm (Haidt & Joseph, 2007), perhaps revealing a kind of confusion that is mitigated by the analytic reasoning fostered by higher education. Likewise, every implementation of the Milgram experiment has found at least a few subjects who refuse to shock (Blass, 1999). Other subjects who do succumb and act badly later regret their actions, triggering a positive change in their moral orientations that outlasts the experimental situation. Any claims about the nature of morality must take these people into account. The behavior of random or representative samples in experimental situations might not be shared by people whose moral understanding and characters are more fully developed—nor by people who are more open to learning. For this reason, inferences based on the limits of typical responses will lead to a distorted view of morality. This is the second, and most important, of the reasons behind our assertion that the study of human development needs exemplar samples.

There is a developmental point here as well. To say that conscious moral choice is not always—or even not usually—involved in behavior should not imply that it is never involved. Many routine moral habits have been worked out during childhood and require no further thought: Ordinary people do not need to consider whether to grab a slice of pizza off someone else's plate when its owner steps out of the room momentarily, though they may have needed to pause and think about this a bit at age 2. Certain situations, though, place people under pressures that routine habits cannot so easily resolve. In those situations, ordinary people may be morally confused or act in ways that are biased by self-interest. But these limitations can be addressed educationally. Phil Zimbardo (who demonstrated a conscious moral judgment of his own by stopping his experiment when it became apparent that it was provoking cruel behavior) has since launched a "Heroic Imagination Project" dedicated to building the capacity of individuals to resist the demands of situations that pressure people to act immorally. This new work relies on the promise of education to help people learn to do better, and it draws on the promise of human development to enable people to grow beyond their base biological inheritance.

The social psychological, biological, and economic lines of work that we have discussed cannot capture the complex reality of moral behavior in its full human sense, in part because of the methodological limitations of such work, and in part because of its impoverished theoretical vision. The deterministic vision of these studies discounts beliefs, choices, and ideals that have moved highly developed people to moral action throughout recorded history. Many who have been moved by elevated moral ideals have sacrificed their own interests, thrown themselves into the breach during battles, transcended their desire for revenge to make peace with their enemies, and handed over large shares of their wealth to others. Many have dedicated extended periods of their lives to pursuing moral purposes centered on peace, justice, love for humanity, and the well-being of others. Research paradigms that fail to examine and account for people like this are extrapolating from the limitations of ordinary people to the nature of morality itself. This false inference is like concluding that there is no such thing as rigorous analytical thinking on the grounds that most people exhibit fallacious reasoning in studies of systematic cognitive bias (Tversky, 1974). To show how one might correct for the sampling biases that lead to such a distorted view, we turn to the exemplar methodology.

Moral Formation in Exemplary 20th Century Leaders

For the past 40 years, the two authors of this chapter have been trying to understand a mysterious, sometimes fragile, but undeniably central part of human development—the moral commitment of people who dedicate their lives to goals that represent moral principles. Our present work explores the lives of seven exemplary leaders from the 20th century: Jane Addams, Dietrich Bonhoeffer, Dag Hammarskjold, Abraham Heschel, Pope John Paul II, Nelson Mandela, and Eleanor Roosevelt. In this study, we are investigating the roles that humility, truth, and faith play in the moral formation and functioning of these exceptional moral leaders. Each of the seven withstood situational pressures, actively questioned and responded to unjust or inhumane cultural norms, reflected on and reshaped their own base impulses and weaknesses of character, and tried to live in the light of transcendent ideals that ennoble the frail human condition. By looking at their lives and their own understandings of their challenges and aspirations, we are attempting to describe the dynamics of moral courage, commitment, and leadership.

For example, former South African president Nelson Mandela not only survived unbroken 27 years of brutal confinement in South African prisons, he also found ways to pursue human rights and social justice even during his confinement. Toward the end of his imprisonment, Mandela had become such a powerful international symbol of justice and courage that the South African authorities wanted to release him to stanch the negative world attention he was drawing to them. But even after decades of suffering, Mandela refused the offer of release unless his conditions were met, conditions that included the freedom to pursue his political agenda in whatever ways he believed were needed and the release of other prisoners who were being held without legitimate cause. This refusal was costly, and he remained in prison for several years on the basis of his principled stand. Eventually, Mandela was able to negotiate a release on his own terms and, once released, stunned the world with his generosity of spirit and his commitment to reconciliation with his oppressors. Mandela understood that hatred and revenge would undermine the possibilities for national harmony, as well as for justice and liberation of the oppressed. His total commitment to justice for all, not just his own people, and to the need for harmony and inclusiveness in his deeply divided country, enabled him to bring people together at a time when that seemed virtually impossible.

When Nelson Mandela became South Africa's first post-apartheid president, his capacity to forgive and his desire to heal his nation led to truly exceptional moral creativity. In the face of horrific offenses against his people, Mandela instituted a strategy for national healing that was original, counterintuitive, risky, and controversial. To resolve the legacy of grievances committed under decades of apartheid rule, President Mandela worked with his long-term colleague and friend, Bishop Desmond Tutu, to establish a Truth and Reconciliation Commission (TRC) that departed radically from the Nuremburg model that the Allies used to prosecute Nazi war crimes after World War II. The purpose of the TRC was to allow perpetrators on all sides of the conflict to acknowledge and take responsibility for past wrongdoing. To this end, the forum was opened to accused and accusers alike, and amnesty was liberally used to elicit frank confessions. Although its de-emphasis on criminal prosecutions was understandably controversial among apartheid's victims and their families, the TRC has been widely recognized for bringing out the full scope of human rights violations that had occurred under the previous regime. It led to confessions, apologies, and statements of regret by perpetrators that made possible the beginnings of productive dialogues, a large step toward national healing and the eventual national unity. The TRC model has been adopted in over 20 countries since its use in South Africa during the 1990s.

Mandela is but one recent shining example in history's pantheon of moral leaders. Every society honors those who have shown courage, commitment, integrity, and moral imagination in service to the common good. Another of our 20th century exemplars is Eleanor Roosevelt, who was for many years the most widely admired woman in the world. The child of a privileged, politically prominent American family, Roosevelt spent her life working to bring about greater justice for working people, women, minorities, and the poor. She pursued this agenda relentlessly, before, during, and after the 12 years she spent as First Lady during the presidency of her husband, Franklin Delano Roosevelt.

Like the other six people we are studying, Roosevelt's moral leadership was based on a commitment to noble purposes transcending her own self-interests. A glimpse into this aspect of Roosevelt's character has been provided by Mary Ann Glendon, who noted, "In an era conspicuous for the self-interest of both nations and individuals, she has become more and more widely recognized as a person of towering unselfishness . . . Mrs. Roosevelt never cares if there is nothing in it for herself. She has absolutely no pride of station and no personal ambition. [To many], she is the personification of the American conscience" (Glendon, 2001, p. 206).

Ordinary people, too, sometimes show such elevated qualities, even if in less heroic and celebrated ways. People the world over love and care for others, both within their own families and well beyond. They dedicate themselves to their work and try to do it in ways that are socially respon-sible. They help people in need without expecting recognition or reward. Some even risk their lives to rescue strangers. This kind of vital moral force cannot be explained by a science that reduces morality to biological im-pulses, situational pressures, or economic self-interest.

In our earlier study of 23 living moral exemplars, we found strong de-grees of integration between self and moral concerns (Colby & Damon, 1992), and we concluded from this that moral commitment involves a "uniting of self and morality": As we wrote at the time, "People who define themselves in terms of their moral goals are likely to see moral problems in everyday events, and they are also likely to see themselves as necessarily implicated in these problems. From there, it is but a small step to taking re-sponsibility for the solution" (Colby & Damon, 1992, p. 307). People differ in the degree to which they define themselves in terms of moral concerns and aims. In one study, Walker and his colleagues found that "morality had differing degrees of centrality in people's identities: For some, moral con-siderations and issues were pervasive in their experience because morality was rooted in the heart of their being; for others, moral issues seemed re-mote, and moral values and standards were not basic to their self-concept" (Walker, Pitts, Hennig, & Matsuba, 1995, p. 398).

Our present study builds on our previous work to investigate more fully the phenomenon of moral leadership, including the relationships between moral commitment and moral ideals, self-reflection and intentional man-agement of morally ambiguous personal qualities, and the ways that moral ideas and reflection shape moral emotions. Among other things, our case studies show how most of these moral leaders began adulthood not only with positive moral impulses, but also with moral impulses and emotions that had a darker side. For example, Nelson Mandela as a young man was fearless in defying authorities and prone to uncontrolled anger and reck-lessness that not only undermined constructive action, but also placed him and others at serious risk. As Mandela worked to advance his moral goals in the face of almost overwhelming challenges while in prison, he learned to modulate and harness his emotions so that his exceptional courage and power served a consistently disciplined purposefulness (Meredith, 1997).

Haidt and his colleagues (Haidt, 2007; Haidt & Joseph, 2007) acknowl-edge that innate impulses and concerns are initially unformed to a signifi-cant extent and are shaped through experience. They stress the importance of cultural narratives as especially powerful in shaping individuals' moral reactions, with the implication that adult morality results from the ways that people's cultural and individual contexts mold their inborn moral in-tuitions or inclinations. But these essentially deterministic and relativist frameworks do not adequately take into account the degree to which in-dividuals actively process the narratives they encounter. Exemplar samples are especially valuable for illuminating the ways that thoughtful and cre-ative individuals analyze and evaluate their culture's dominant narratives and question the assumptions of narratives that reinforce injustice. Mandela not only saw through and opposed the dominant narrative of White superiority in South Africa, but he also abandoned the opposing Africanist narrative in favor of a multiracial approach.

For Mandela, this process began in childhood and adolescence and continued into and beyond middle age. Mandela grew up in a country that consciously and severely disempowered Black Africans, subjecting them to constant humiliation and injustice. But he also grew up aware that his family was descended from a line of tribal chieftains and, as a boy, he was fascinated by stories of native freedom fighters, whose powerful spirit he admired and tried to emulate. Mandela's sense of dignity and noble heritage, evident from adolescence onward, strengthened his capacity to resist White domination but also led him to take potentially disastrous risks.

A turning point for the young Mandela came when he took part in a protest while a student at the South African Native College at Fort Hare. Graduation from this elite institution assured success in any career then open to Africans. But Mandela gave up this secure future by refusing to back away from the protest when threatened with expulsion. Instead, Mandela and another student ran away to Johannesburg with no money, credentials, or contacts. This might have been a tale of dramatic downward mobility, but through extraordinary resourcefulness the young Mandela worked his way into a law practice through which he managed to complete his undergraduate and legal studies.

At that point, Mandela again chose not to pursue a relatively comfortable life as one of the country's few Black professionals, turning instead to legal and political resistance to apartheid. At each of the major turning points in his astonishing life, Mandela made choices that were driven by his developing ideals. Even when he didn't seem to be relying on deductive or calculative thinking to reach moral conclusions, the driving forces of his life were his particular formulations of the moral ideals of human dignity, freedom, fairness, social harmony, and individual responsibility. Mandela had begun to develop these ideals in adolescence and continued to refine them as his experience expanded, further deepening his understanding and commitment.

Others in our sample of seven moral leaders also showed early signs of promise, combined with notable turning points, which were driven to a great extent by their own reflection on and redefinition of their ideals. Eleanor Roosevelt's parents had both died when she was very young and she grew up a timid child, entirely lacking in self-confidence. After living for a while with a harsh grandmother who further undermined her confidence, Eleanor was sent to boarding school in the United Kingdom. This was a critical juncture for her. When the school's highly committed, thoughtful, and sophisticated headmistress, Madame Marie Souvestre, took her new student under her wing, Eleanor's transformation into one of the great feminist leaders of the 20th century began to unfold. Souvestre's confidence in Eleanor, combined with the intellectual and moral guidance she provided, was critical in setting the adolescent girl on a new and, ultimately, remarkable life path.

Both formal and informal educational experiences were influential for the young Jane Addams as well, another in our group of seven moral leaders. When Addams won the Nobel Peace Prize in 1931, she was known the world over for her pioneering social reform efforts at a time that the United States was undergoing massive industrialization and struggling to incorporate huge numbers of immigrants. She was a leader in campaigns to improve conditions for workers, protect free speech and other civil liberties, secure the rights of women, and foster world peace. Addams was a central figure in the great wave of social reforms that transformed American life during the first decades of the 20th century, a period that became known as the Progressive Era. She was co-founder of the best-known and most influential settlement house in American history, Hull House, and was also involved in the founding of the Women's International League for Peace and Freedom and several other important human rights organizations in the United States. Addams was a prolific writer, especially in the emerging field of applied sociology, and her work influenced and drew together many prominent intellectuals of her time, including John Dewey, the great educational philosopher.

Growing up in a family for which moral duty was a central value, Jane was a serious child and adolescent. She was a voracious reader, devouring books about moral heroism, women's history, religion, and moral philosophy. She also immersed herself in Charles Dickens's vividly humane portrayals of society's outcasts, acquiring from them her lasting desire to live among the poor and find ways to relieve their suffering. At college, Addams was inspired by a humanities teacher, Caroline Potter, whose courses she took in every one of her four years. According to Addams's biographer, Louise Knight, "Potter's entire curriculum was an intense and lengthy seminar on the heroic, and Jane was entranced" (Knight, 2010, p. 23).

Despite the inspiration she felt, Jane struggled to find her way. Like Eleanor Roosevelt, she had lost her mother when she was a child, and her father died when she was a young adult. Although she longed to do something worthwhile with her life, the death of her beloved father left Jane overcome with grief. Feeling weak and helpless, she despaired of ever finding something to which she could really commit herself, crying out, "How purposeless and without ambition I am!"

Jane saw no way out of her malaise, and the restrictive culture of her day offered no help. Women of her class were discouraged from pursuing careers or social causes beyond simple charity work. But, during a trip to Europe in which she was shocked by the squalor and suffering she saw, Jane came across a new approach to urban poverty in a settlement house in London called Toynbee Hall. This democratic Christian community, in which well educated people lived among the poor and worked to enhance the lives of the poor and privileged alike, was the master idea that would lead her to the fruitful pathway that had so far eluded her, giving her a purpose and direction from which she never deviated.

The result was a life of exceptional moral creativity. In her long career, Addams developed and practiced new approaches to democracy based in solidarity across class, gender, and ethnic lines. In doing so, she not only renounced the standard roles and attitudes of women of her privileged station in the early 20th century United States, but she also radically redefined previously unquestioned moral ideals. Although Addams had grown up in a family that was dedicated to the ideal of benevolence, she came to see benevolence as a condescending, selfish, arrogant, anti-democratic ethic that needed to be set aside in favor of truly democratic community building. This conceptual reformulation of Addams's central moral ideal informed and was informed by her long-term efforts to respond to the massive industrialization and immigration that were disrupting the country and to advance civil rights, woman suffrage, peace, and equitable conditions for workers.

Critics of theories that emphasize the role of cognition in moral development portray moral thinking as post-hoc rationalization, and they interpret the relative infrequency of deliberate analysis in decision making as evidence for an intuitionist theory of morality. But a close look at the lives of recognized moral leaders reveals a more subtle and bidirectional process of moral reflection as it interacts with moral conduct and experience over time. This is not intellectualizing in a vacuum. It is an active, ongoing process of reflection about one's life and experiences, drawing on ideas, stories, images, and critical capacities, and it can lead to the creation and refinement of the person's moral ideals and understandings. Moral reflection of this kind can establish foundational ideas that strongly influence the actual choices a person makes. Over time, these foundational ideas become so engrained in the individual's way of seeing the world that they appear to operate automatically, almost like intuitive responses, and thus affect individuals' choices even when they need to be made quickly and under duress.

This developmental process of reflection on and reformulation of ideals can be supported by educational efforts that are designed to foster moral learning. When teachers and other adults stimulate young people's reflections about the kinds of persons they want to be and the kinds of lives they want to live, young people can acquire the will and the capacity to bring their conscious moral judgments to bear on their behavioral choices. This kind of education begins with the assumption that students are not passive recipients of socialization. They can benefit from support and guidance, and with such guidance they are capable of making their own moral meaning and their own moral choices.

The stories of our seven moral leaders illustrate the sense in which the perspective on human development that emerges from studies with exemplar samples is, above all, a hopeful view. It is surely true, as the biological, social psychological, and economic lenses on humanity suggest, that many people are morally confused or driven to a large extent by self-interest, especially under situational pressures. But exemplar studies begin from the assumption that social scientists need to include the most mature in their samples if they are to understand the true scope of morality. These studies are based in a belief that all can aspire to more elevated selves, and they document the fact that many people do achieve this goal. This developmentally grounded hope forms the basis for educational programs that support the growth of integrity, clarity of thought and judgment, and lives informed by a positive sense of purpose. A determinedly descriptive approach is not adequate for a scientific understanding of morality, or for a popular understanding of this critically important dimension of human life. And an exclusively descriptive approach is seriously deficient as the basis for education and human improvement. As Narvaez (2006) has argued, moral education requires us to stake normative claims about what we believe is right and worthy of being passed on. Without some sense of what constitutes a more worthy and inspiring ideal, we cannot even select an exemplar sample, let alone learn from exemplars' lives in order to improve our own.

References

Atlas, J. (2012, May 13). The amygdala made me do it. *New York Times*, p. B1.

Blass, T. (1999). The Milgram paradigm after 35 years: Some things we now know about obedience to authority. *Journal of Applied Social Psychology, 29*(5), 955–978.

Colby, A., & Damon, W. (1992). *Some do care: Contemporary lives of moral commitment.* New York, NY: Free Press.

Gardner, H. (1983). *Frames of mind: The theory of multiple intelligences.* New York, NY: Basic Books.

Gardner, H. (2006). *Multiple intelligences: New horizons in theory and practice.* New York, NY: Basic Books.

Gardner, H. (2011). *Truth, beauty, and goodness reframed: Educating for the virtues in the 21st century.* New York, NY: Basic Books.

Glendon, M. A. (2001). *A world made new: Eleanor Roosevelt and the declaration of human rights.* New York, NY: Random House.

Haidt, J. (2007). The new synthesis in moral psychology. *Science, 316,* 998–1002.

Haidt, J., & Joseph, C. (2007). The moral mind: How 5 sets of innate moral intuitions guide the development of many culture-specific virtues, and perhaps even modules. In P. Carruthers, S. Laurence, & S. Stich (Eds.), *The innate mind* (Vol. 3, pp. 367–391). New York, NY: Oxford University Press.

Hartshorne, H., & May, M. (1928). *Studies in the nature of character. Vol 1: Deceit.* New York, NY: Macmillan.

Hauser, M. (2006). *Moral minds: How nature designed our universal sense of right and wrong.* New York, NY: Ecco.

Kahneman, D. (2011). *Thinking, fast and slow.* New York, NY: Farrar, Straus and Giroux.

Knight, L. (2010). *Jane Addams: Spirit in action.* New York, NY: Norton & Company.

Kolm, S., & Ythier, J. M. (Eds.). (2006). *Handbook of the economics of giving, altruism and reciprocity* (Vol. 1, no. 1). Philadelphia, PA: Elsevier.

Latane, B., & Darley, J. (1969). Bystander "apathy." *American Scientist, 57,* 244–268.

Meredith, M. (1997). *Mandela: A biography*. New York, NY: Public Affairs.

Milgram, S. (1974). *Obedience to authority: An experimental view*. Cambridge, MA: Harvard University Press.

Narvaez, D. (2006). Integrative ethical education. In M. Killen & J. Smetana (Eds.), *Handbook of moral development* (pp. 703–733). Mahwah, NJ: Erlbaum.

Piaget, J. (1970). Piaget's theory. In P. Mussen (Ed.), *Carmichael's manual of child psychology* (Vol. 1). New York, NY: Wiley.

Tversky, A. (1974). Judgment under uncertainty: Heuristics and biases. *Science, 185,* 1124–1131.

Walker, L., Pitts, R., Hennig, K., & Matsuba, M. (1995). Reasoning about morality and real-life moral problems. In M. Killen & D. Hart (Eds.), *Morality in everyday life* (pp. 371–407). New York, NY: Cambridge University Press.

Zimbardo, P. (2007). *The Lucifer effect: Understanding how good people turn evil*. New York, NY: Random House.

WILLIAM DAMON *is a professor of education at Stanford University and the director of the Stanford Center on Adolescence.*

ANNE COLBY *is a consulting professor at Stanford University.*

NEW DIRECTIONS FOR CHILD AND ADOLESCENT DEVELOPMENT • DOI: 10.1002/cad

Walker, L. J. (2013). Exemplars' moral behavior is self-regarding. In M. K. Matsuba, P. E. King, & K. C. Bronk (Eds.), *Exemplar methods and research: Strategies for investigation*. New Directions for Child and Adolescent Development, 142, 27–40.

3

Exemplars' Moral Behavior Is Self-Regarding

Lawrence J. Walker

Abstract

What fundamentally motivates moral behavior? What is the nature and source of moral motivation? The argument developed in this chapter is that moral action is not merely other-regarding; it also can, and should be, self-regarding. When there is something significant for the self in the moral enterprise, it can legitimately be self-enhancing and, thus, powerfully motivating. The empirical warrant for this argument is found in the study of the psychological functioning of moral exemplars. The research reviewed here indicates that moral exemplars do synergistically integrate their self-promoting agentic motivation in service to their other-promoting communal values. Therein is the powerful motivational impetus for doing good and living rightly. © 2013 Wiley Periodicals, Inc.

A recalcitrant issue that scholars in the field of moral development have struggled to resolve, without obvious success, centers on the source and nature of moral motivation: Why, exactly, should we do good and live rightly? What psychological mechanisms actually engender moral behavior? Many theories espouse lofty ideals of principled rationality or selfless sacrifice, but notably lack traction because the means for the realization of these ideals are left unspecified or are psychologically unrealistic. The issue of the source and nature of moral motivation is important because it speaks to the boundaries of how we conceptualize the moral domain, to the viability of the processes we use to explain moral development and functioning, and to the efficacy of our socialization and intervention efforts. So much hinges on the issue of moral motivation.

The argument developed in this chapter is that morality can, and indeed should, be self-regarding, not merely other-regarding. In other words, there should be something significant for one's self in the enterprise—moral behavior can legitimately be self-enhancing and self-promoting. If that is the case, then there is powerful motivational impetus for doing good and living rightly. The empirical warrant for this conceptual argument has, in my recent program of research, been constructed largely through the psychological study of moral exemplars—extraordinary people who live out many of our ethical ideals.

Why Study Moral Exemplars?

It may be helpful to mount the case for studying moral exemplars. It certainly is not the most expedient approach to research but, as it turns out, it does yield considerable dividends in the end.

Real-World Behaviors. Exemplars are identified, typically through some process of social consensus, for engaging in notable moral behaviors. These behaviors are meaningful, significant, and enacted in the real world; as such, they have considerable face validity. Contrast such behaviors with the often contrived moral (or immoral) behaviors that are often elicited in laboratory or experimental contexts. Moral exemplars are valued research participants because, as persons, they have convincingly engaged in the behaviors of primary interest.

Expanding the Moral Domain. For a long time, research on morality has been driven by various conceptual skews because theorists have reified single variables as core to the moral domain, thereby ignoring or minimizing other relevant aspects. This has led to a constricted and distorted understanding of the breadth and complexity of moral functioning. Kohlberg's (1981) explicit emphasis on justice and moral rationality is illustrative of one such conceptual skew, as is Gilligan's (1982) advocacy for an ethic of care, Hoffman's (2000) focus on empathy, and so on. Morality is too complicated and multifaceted to be adequately explained by single variables. Scholars are, of course, rightly partial to their favored theoretical perspectives, but a helpful way to reduce this bias is to examine the psychological functioning of real people who are exemplars of morality. This approach can draw attention to aspects of moral functioning that may have been previously overlooked.

Extreme Groups Amplify Effects. When the psychological functioning of exemplars is contrasted with that of ordinary folk (or an even more acute contrast with exemplars of immorality), such group comparisons, based on relatively extreme groups, can serve to amplify differences and so be more clearly indicative of many operative processes in moral functioning. Because of the rarity of exemplars (by definition), some researchers rely on qualitative methods and do not include comparison groups, making inferences somewhat tenuous. And, obviously, people cannot be randomly assigned to exemplar and control groups, as in an experiment, so the construction of comparison groups in exemplar research does have its methodological challenges, which should be kept in mind. Essentially, individuals in a comparison group should be as closely matched as possible to those in the exemplar group, so that the operative variables in moral functioning can be more easily discerned. Matching on demographic variables may not, for example, be sufficient to ensure comparability on social or psychological variables (see Frimer, Walker, Lee, Riches, & Dunlop [2012] for an elaboration of this point), so researchers need to be alert for confounding variables and attempt to surmount them whenever possible.

Person-Level Analyses. Although not a requisite for exemplar research, broadband assessments of exemplars' psychological functioning are often obtained. Given the difficulty in accessing exemplar participants, researchers frequently make the most of their efforts by using multiple measures to tap a range of potentially relevant variables; the dataset is frequently extensive. This methodological approach not only has the potential to expand the psychological boundaries of the moral domain, but it can also yield more holistic understandings through reliance on within-person analyses. In contrast to the traditional variable-level analytic strategy, a person-level approach examines the phenomenologically real interaction among variables within the person, which is more revelatory of functional psychological dynamics (Magnusson, 2003), as will be illustrated later.

Reverse Engineering. A focus on morally mature exemplars represents a research strategy of reverse engineering wherein a fully functioning, finished "product" is obtained and then progressively deconstructed in order to discover its operative mechanisms. In the context of moral exemplars, the process of reverse engineering first entails gaining an understanding of the psychological dynamics implicated in moral maturity and, then, working backward to figure out developmental trajectories and causal factors.

Ethical Ideals. Psychological research with moral exemplars can inform our ethical ideals by indicating what is humanly attainable and what forms they may take. As Flanagan (1991) has argued, moral theory must be grounded in human psychology or else we are condemned to a tyrant's morality. The issues here include, for example, whether there is a singular form of moral excellence or there exist multiple forms that are equally viable and appropriate. Are there different ways to be good? And do at least super-ficially different types of moral exemplars share some common attributes that define a foundational core of morality?

Of course, the notion that there might be different types of moral exem-plars should be considered in light of the adage that one person's saint can be another's scoundrel. Might the existence of different types of moral "heroes" simply be a reflection of the different moralities that are extant across groups? Haidt and Graham (2007) contend, for example, that political lib-erals are attuned to the moral foundations of care and fairness, whereas con-servatives rely more broadly on the five foundations of care, fairness, loy-alty, authority, and purity. In a test of this notion, Frimer, Biesanz, Walker, and MacKinlay (2013) examined the moral evaluations made by liberals and conservatives of a set of highly renowned people (drawn from *Time* magazine's lists of the most influential people of the past century, including leaders, revolutionaries, heroes, and icons) and found that consensus be-tween ideologies was the norm and that controversial (or "wedge") figures were relatively rare, implying a largely uniform and shared notion of moral exemplarity even in the context of contemporary "culture wars."

In this introductory section, the case has been set out for studying moral exemplars. I now turn to expand upon the core argument of this chapter: that morality can be self-regarding.

Appropriating Morality

What fundamentally motivates moral behavior? What is the nature and source of moral motivation? Many extant theories do not have a ready an-swer because they ignore or disparage the role of the self in moral func-tioning. This failure is manifested variously: by denigration of notions of character (Kohlberg, 1981), by segregating the personal from the moral do-main (Turiel, 1983), by advancing constructs of self-denying altruism and empathy (de Waal, 2009; Hoffman, 2000), and by defining morality as sur-mounting selfishness (Haidt, 2008). The implicit (and sometimes explicit) argument in these theories is that morality should not be self-regarding—it would be unseemly to even countenance that, an apparent contradiction in terms. One's moral mandate is to overcome personal interests by engaging in drear duty, onerous obligation, and selfless sacrifice. This all implies, of course, that others' interests are ethically prior to one's own; that there is no moral credit in promoting one's own interests and welfare. Such theo-ries exacerbate the problem by implicitly positing an inert view of moral motivation.

Flanagan (1991) helpfully offers a contrary, more eudaimonic perspec-tive: As humans, he argues, we are rightly partial to our own projects and interests, which impart meaning to life and, indeed, this meaning is integral to, and constitutive of, morality. He further contends, as a form of "reality check," that ethical theories, in order to be considered viable, should specify a psychologically realistic motivational mechanism for the actualization of their ideals.

My argument is that the developing appropriation of morality to the self is such a mechanism—one which has motivational force because, once in place, morality becomes self-regarding. Under such conditions, acting on moral concerns is, thus, self-enhancing, while failing to do so is self-defeating. Blasi (1983) and Damon (1984) can be credited with foundational arguments along these lines, particularly for advancing the relevance of concepts related to the moral self. Among the various concepts posited are notions of psychological self-consistency, personal responsibility, moral centrality (to identity), integrity of identity, willpower, and moral desires. Unfortunately, with the exception of moral centrality (for a discussion, see Walker, in press), these notions have not been adequately operationalized and so have garnered minimal empirical support.

The first suggestive evidence that morality can be self-regarding was reported by Colby and Damon (1992) in their case-study analysis of a small sample of moral exemplars who were involved in social action. They observed that their exemplars seemingly had a coherent identity that meaningfully integrated the personal and moral aspects of their lives. For these exemplars, moral action was not an exercise in self-sacrifice, nor the outcome of heady dilemmatic deliberation. Rather, exemplars garnered personal fulfillment from advancing their prosocial projects. Moral concerns and action were endemic to their personalities. Intimations of similar themes can be discerned in other qualitative studies of moral exemplars (Oliner, 2003; Reimer, 2009), but the lack of objective methodology and appropriate comparison groups renders such conclusions unsubstantiated.

Notions of Moral Exemplarity

Although the focus of this chapter is on the motivational functioning of moral exemplars, research on conceptions of moral exemplarity can be heuristic in pointing to critical variables. After all, studying moral exemplars first requires an understanding of what, exactly, we might mean by moral excellence. The notions of moral exemplarity proffered by ordinary folk may not be as nuanced and sophisticated as those of experts who are guided by philosophical considerations, but lay notions are probably better representative of what is actually operative in everyday life and can be revelatory of extant conceptual skews.

Walker and Pitts (1998) derived a taxonomy of moral exemplarity using a multi-study procedure. In an initial study, adult participants generated (by freely listing) the traits of a highly moral person. From this voluminous output, a nonredundant set of frequently identified traits was constructed which, in a second study, adult participants then rated for prototypicality. In a third study, college student participants organized the most prototypic of these traits into groups (by similarity sorting). The data-reduction technique of multidimensional scaling was used to identify the dimensions underlying participants' conceptions. The primary dimension was identified as a self/other dimension, whereas the secondary dimension was external/internal in nature. The traits along the self/other dimension ranged from self-referential agentic ones at one end, to other-focused communal ones at the other end. The external/internal dimension referenced external standards and norms for moral behavior versus internal aspects of conscience.

Walker and Pitts's (1998) studies were conducted with adults, leaving developmental questions unaddressed. Interestingly, Hardy, Walker, Olsen, Skalski, and Basinger (2011) found that the same two dimensions organized adolescents' understandings of moral exemplarity. Further, Walker and Hennig (2004) examined conceptions of different types of moral exemplarity (just, brave, caring) and found the same dimensional tension between agentic and communal traits across these disparate types.

Thus, a major finding from research on conceptions of moral exemplarity is that they clearly reference the relationship between self and other, between agency and communion (the fundamental motivational duality) (Bakan, 1966), signaling its centrality in moral functioning. But with these data, the form of the relationship remains ambiguous: Do people think that some exemplars are agentic and other exemplars are communal? Or do they think that these motivations are in acute tension for exemplars? Or, in accord with my argument, do they think that exemplars have integrated their self-regarding agentic and other-regarding communal motivation? To address that critical question, we must turn to research on actual exemplars.

Situational Challenge

Before focusing on research examining the motivational profile of moral exemplars, we need to confront the situational challenge that anybody can be a moral hero if the circumstances are conducive (Zimbardo, 2007). The situational perspective in social psychology (Doris, 2002) discounts any causal significance to dispositional factors, such as motivation, and contends instead that contextual factors are primary in instigating moral behavior. In contrast, the dispositional perspective, which better frames our program of research, assumes that motivational aspects of character are causally operative in moral action. So there you have it: a contest between context and character.

Walker, Frimer, and Dunlop (2010) addressed this issue by examining the personalities of moral exemplars and comparison participants. The exemplars were recipients of national (Canadian) awards for extraordinary moral action (the Medal of Bravery and the Caring Canadian Award), and the comparison participants were demographically matched on a case-by-case basis. Participants responded to a broadband assessment of their personality using multiple measures. The situational perspective holds that contextual factors instigate moral action, so it predicts no meaningful differences between so-called exemplars and comparisons in motivation and personality functioning.

The dispositional perspective, on the other hand, does predict that differences will be revealed between exemplars and comparisons—that is, that moral motivation is a viable explanatory construct—but there are differing predictions regarding the number and nature of these dispositions. For example, Aristotle's (trans. 1962) notion of the unity of the virtues implies a single type of exemplary disposition, with the full array of (interdependent) virtues apparent. Kohlberg's (1981) position similarly advocates for a single type, but instead frames by the single variable of moral reasoning ("virtue is not many, but one, and its name is justice," p. 39). In contrast to both Aristotle and Kohlberg, Flanagan (1991) contends that there are multiple varieties of moral exemplarity, each distinctive and partial in its composition; that virtue can legitimately be manifest in qualitatively different ways.

A cluster analysis of the exemplars, based on the broadband assessment of their personalities, revealed three distinctive clusters indicative of different modes of moral motivation. This finding accords with Flanagan's notion of varieties of moral exemplarity and is inconsistent with both Aristotle's and Kohlberg's singular visions. Two of the exemplar clusters (a "communal" cluster and a "deliberative" one, labeled according to the variables characterizing them) were strongly distinguished from their matched comparison groups, supporting the perspective that character is implicated in moral action. Interestingly, the third cluster of exemplars (labeled "ordinary") had a personality profile that was uniformly banal in comparison to other exemplars and indistinguishable from their comparison group, a finding that accords with the situational perspective.

Thus, this study provided consolation to both the dispositional and the situational perspectives. Upon further investigation, it was apparent that the communal and deliberative clusters were populated primarily by caring award recipients (who had been committed to long-term volunteer service), whereas the ordinary cluster was populated primarily by bravery award recipients (who had engaged in one-off heroic rescues). This pattern resonates with Fleeson's (2004) resolution of the person × situation issue: Momentary behaviors are often better explained by contextual factors, whereas long-term patterns of behavior (the "moral career") are better explained by characterological factors.

Moral Core

Having garnered some support for the dispositional notion of moral character, the question now turns to what are the foundational variables, relevant to morality, to which we should attend. The research strategy ideally entails casting a wide net—a comprehensive and broadband assessment of psychological functioning.

Matsuba and Walker (2004, 2005) were among the first to enact this research strategy, assessing moral exemplars at all levels of personality description—behavioral traits, characteristic adaptations, and integrative life narratives (see McAdams [1995] for an explication of this comprehensive typology of personality description). In Matsuba and Walker's studies, exemplars were young adults who had been identified for their extraordinary efforts in social service agencies; a matched comparison group was also recruited. Results indicated these young adult exemplars were characterized by several variables: traits of agreeableness, an other-model of attachment, prosocial goals, recollections of others' suffering, advanced ego-identity status, mature moral reasoning and epistemic development, ideological depth, and themes of agency. Note that this set of variables clearly includes elements of both agentic and communal motivation.

Matsuba and Walker's exemplars were young adults who were just embarking upon their moral careers, so it is possible that operative processes were not fully apparent. Walker and Frimer (2007) recruited a sample of more notable exemplars who had received national awards for their moral action: brave exemplars who had risked their lives to save others and caring exemplars who had engaged in extraordinary volunteer service. In trying to identify the foundational core of moral functioning, the analytic strategy taken here was to determine which variables, across the wide range assessed, were shared by the two disparate types of moral exemplarity (brave vs. caring) and which also distinguished each from their respective comparison groups. The results indicated that the common core of moral exemplarity entailed formative and beneficial relationships in childhood, redemptive construals of critical life events in which some benefit is discerned out of negative experiences (McAdams, 2006), and stronger themes of both agency and communion. Note that both brave and caring exemplars were both strongly agentic and communal (not that the brave exemplars were agentic and the caring exemplars were communal).

Subsequent analyses with this dataset (Dunlop, Walker, & Matsuba, 2012) addressed the question of whether the moral personality of caring exemplars would emerge from the data without any prior group classification. Dunlop and colleagues (2012) conducted a cluster analysis of the exemplar and comparison participants, based on the comprehensive set of personality variables, and found that two clusters were identified: one largely comprised exemplars, the other, comparisons. In other words, the distinctive moral personality of caring exemplars emerged from the data. Dunlop and Walker (2013) conducted the same type of analysis with the brave exemplar and comparison participants and, again, the distinctive moral personality of brave exemplars was apparent. Although unique personality profiles were revealed for the caring and brave exemplars, both entailed the hallmarks of both agentic and communal motivation. Any way you slice it, both agency and communion feature prominently in the psychological functioning of moral exemplars.

Synergistic Integration of Agency and Communion

That both agency and communion are hallmarks of moral exemplarity points to the psychological mechanism of aligning and reconciling the interests of self and other in moral functioning. As noted earlier, these themes are also ubiquitous in naturalistic conceptions of moral exemplarity (Hardy et al., 2011; Walker & Hennig, 2004; Walker & Pitts, 1998). Agency and communion are fundamental themes in motivation (Bakan, 1966), where they are often conceptualized as antagonistic and mutually interfering (e.g., Hogan [1982] describes these motives as "getting ahead" and "getting along" and Schwartz et al. [2012] place these motives on opposing sides of the values circumplex).

The reconciliation model (Frimer & Walker, 2009), however, frames the relationship between these motives developmentally. It proposes that, in childhood and adolescence, these motives develop largely in segregation, eventually increasing sufficiently in strength until they begin to "butt heads" at a motivational turning point. This motivational tension can be resolved in a number of ways: the flagging of motivation in general, the attenuation of one motive and the ascendance of the other (resulting in either unmitigated agency or unmitigated communion, both of which are problematic motivational states), or their integration. Thus, the model posits the possible developmental transition in these motives from being independent and competing to being interdependent and synergistic. The consistent pattern of findings of accentuated levels of both agentic and communal motivation in the psychological functioning of moral exemplars is certainly suggestive of their synergistic interaction.

But these strong themes of both agency and communion could simply indicate that exemplars are strongly motivated in general. The critical question is whether there is any evidence of a synergistic interaction between these motives in moral maturity, evidence which would bolster the notion that morality can be both self- and other-regarding. In an initial test of this notion of a synergistic interaction (an effect that is greater than the sum of its parts), Walker and Frimer (2007) examined the relationship between agency and communion in their sample of national award exemplars and comparison participants. As noted before, exemplars evidenced stronger themes of both agency and communion than did comparison participants. In Walker and Frimer's analysis, however, once levels of agency and communion were accounted for, there was no evidence of a statistical interaction between the variables, failing to support the notion of synergy.

Not to be thwarted, however, Frimer, Walker, Dunlop, Lee, and Riches (2011) revisited the issue with the same dataset. First, they introduced a conceptual clarification of the meaning of agency and communion. Many definitions of these motives abound with considerable variability (Paulhus & Trapnell, 2008), so definitions were adopted that were more in accord with our own theorizing, with agency framed as self-promoting (motives of power and achievement) and communion as other-promoting (motives of benevolence and universalism). A contrasting definition, for example, focuses more on psychological distance, with agency reflected by individuation and communion by relatedness.

Second, Frimer et al. (2011) introduced an analytical refinement in conducting a person-level analysis rather than the traditional variable-level analysis. In a variable-level analysis (as was conducted by Walker & Frimer, 2007), an interaction is detected based on the overall strength of the variables (even if the individual vacillates between the motives and keeps them segregated); in contrast, in a person-level analysis (Magnusson, 2003), an interaction is detected based on the phenomenologically real co-occurrence of the motives within the person, within the same thought structure. When both the conceptual and analytical refinements were implemented, the synergistic interaction of agency and communion was evident for the moral exemplars, whereas the level of integration found in the comparison group did not differ from what would be expected on the basis of chance; this is the first compelling evidence of the adaptive reconciliation of self-promoting agency and other-promoting communion.

Although Frimer et al.'s (2011) study provided evidence of the integration of agency and communion in moral functioning, an ambiguity remains. That study assessed the co-occurrence of these motives within the individual's thinking on a topic; it did not indicate the directionality between these motives. For example, the co-occurrence of these motives could be of the form of agency promoting communion (e.g., "I'm trying to use my social position to help the poor") or of the form of communion promoting agency (e.g., "I'm involved with this prosocial cause to bolster my social status"). Obviously, different moral credit would be assigned to these two forms. Rokeach (1973) introduced a distinction between instrumental and terminal values. An instrumental value is a means to something else, whereas a terminal value is an end in itself. So, in the example above ("I'm trying to use my social position to help the poor"), the value of one's social position is expressed as being instrumental to the ultimate goal of helping the poor.

Frimer et al. (2012) examined the hierarchical integration of agency and communion in moral motivation by assessing their instrumental–terminal relationship. A different approach to identifying moral exemplars was taken in this study. Rather than recruiting nominees or award recipients for extraordinary moral action, for example, their target subjects were highly influential people of the 20th century, as identified by *Time* magazine at the turn of the millennium. These are the world's most influential leaders, revolutionaries, heroes, and icons—people who have had enormous impact, both positive and negative.

In the first step of their procedure, Frimer et al. (2012) had a large sample of experts rate these target figures on dimensions of moral exemplarity, relying on Colby and Damon's (1992) five criteria for moral excellence (principled/virtuous, consistent, brave, inspiring, and humble). The top-ranking of these figures, based on an overall index of these dimensions, were thus classified as moral exemplars and included such luminaries as Nelson Mandela, Aung San Suu Kyi, Mother Teresa, and Andrei Sakharov. The bottom-ranking of these figures comprised the comparison group of similar influence and included familiar names such as Kim Jong Il, Vladmir Putin, Adolf Hitler, and Marilyn Monroe. The comparison group was a motley one of political leaders, celebrity icons, and athletes, all of some notoriety and all adjudged as not being particularly prototypic of moral excellence.

Obviously, these influential figures were not available for direct participation in research, so their motivational functioning was assessed "at a distance" by systematic content analyses of archival materials (speeches and interviews). Excerpts from these speeches and interviews were first coded for concepts of agency (power, achievement) and communion (benevolence), and then the hierarchical relationship between these motives was assessed by determining which concepts were instrumental to (as a means to) each terminal value (expressed as an end in itself).

The results of these analyses can be encapsulated simply: Comparison figures expressed considerably more agency than communion at both the instrumental and terminal levels—an unequivocal expression of unmitigated agency. Exemplar figures also expressed considerably more agency than communion at the instrumental level; these are highly impactful people, of course. But at the terminal level, communion was indomitable. Exemplars used their agency in promotion of communal causes—the embodiment of enlightened self-interest. This is a perfect illustration of the appropriation of morality to the self, the moral motivational mechanism advanced in this chapter. Morality becomes integral to one's psychological functioning such that personal influence and achievement are fulfilled, and meaning is imparted to life, in an integrated style of motivation by furthering others' welfare.

Conclusion

When morality is framed, as is typical, as an exercise in drear duty, onerous obligation, and selfless sacrifice, it lacks adequate motivational impetus, regardless of the exalted nature of its ideals. Many theories denigrate the role of the self in moral motivation, arguing that virtue entails developing the ability to somehow suppress self-interest in order to do the right thing. In my view, this framing of moral functioning is psychologically quixotic and untenable.

NEW DIRECTIONS FOR CHILD AND ADOLESCENT DEVELOPMENT • DOI: 10.1002/cad

My contention is that morality should not only be other-regarding, but it can, and should also be, self-regarding (in the eudaimonic sense). Such a transformation of moral motivation can be keenly motivating "for creatures like us" (Flanagan, 1991, p. 31). As moral agents, we can capitalize on the power of self-interest by refocusing it so that the self has a meaningful stake in moral action. When moral concerns become core to identity and motivation, then their pursuit is enhancing to the self.

Of course, there are some limitations to this program of research and some future research directions to note. The evidence reviewed in this chapter involved samples drawn from Western contexts. Patterns of agency and communion may well vary between individualistic and collectivistic cultures, so future research should explore cultural variability in the interaction between motives of moral motivation within the instrumental–terminal framing.

Another limitation of this program of research is its reliance on relatively labor-intensive data collection and microanalytic coding procedures. Future research endeavors should explore more expedient methods for obtaining comparable data with reliability and validity.

In this chapter, research was reviewed that, collectively, provides the empirical warrant for the claim that self-promoting agentic motivation is integrated with other-promoting communal motivation in the moral functioning of exemplars. Having demonstrated this motivational mechanism in maturity (the "finished product"), however, begs the next steps in the process of reverse engineering. What are the typical developmental trajectories in moral motivation? And what are the psychological mechanisms that effect divergent trajectories (integration, unmitigated agency, unmitigated communion, continued segregation, or diminished motivation)? How do these various trajectories relate to moral behavior? What is the nature of motivational crisis-points and their manifestation, and how are they typically stoked and resolved? What are the cognitive understandings that contribute to transformations in moral motivation? How do aspects of early socialization of agency and communion (through parenting, community, media, and broader cultural values) influence their developing relationship in adolescence and adulthood? What are the adaptive and maladaptive forms of moral motivation (e.g., pathological altruism) and how can their development best be explained? What are the costs, to both self and others, for engaging in an exemplary moral career? Does it have its shadow or negative side of which we should be aware?

Once causal mechanisms and developmental trajectories in moral motivation have been clarified, then the next step in the process of reverse engineering is to implement and assess intervention efforts. As the adage goes (attributed to Kurt Lewin), "If you want truly to understand something, try to change it."

Why, then, should we do good and live rightly? Simply put, because there's a lot in it for us!

References

Aristotle. (1962). *Nicomachean ethics* (M. Ostwald, Trans.). Indianapolis, IN: Bobbs-Merrill.

Bakan, D. (1966). *The duality of human existence: An essay on psychology and religion.* Chicago, IL: Rand McNally.

Blasi, A. (1983). Moral cognition and moral action: A theoretical perspective. *Developmental Review, 3,* 178–210. doi:10.1016/0273-2297(83)90029-1

Colby, A., & Damon, W. (1992). *Some do care: Contemporary lives of moral commitment.* New York, NY: Free Press.

Damon, W. (1984). Self-understanding and moral development from childhood to adolescence. In W. M. Kurtines & J. L. Gewirtz (Eds.), *Morality, moral behavior, and moral development* (pp. 109–127). New York, NY: Wiley.

de Waal, F. (2009). *The age of empathy: Nature's lessons for a kinder society.* New York, NY: Three Rivers Press.

Doris, J. M. (2002). *Lack of character: Personality and moral behavior.* Cambridge, England: Cambridge University Press.

Dunlop, W. L., & Walker, L. J. (2013). The personality profile of brave exemplars: A person-centered analysis. *Journal of Research in Personality, 47,* 380–384. doi:10.1016/j.jrp.2013.03.004

Dunlop, W. L., Walker, L. J., & Matsuba, M. K. (2012). The distinctive moral personality of care exemplars. *Journal of Positive Psychology, 7,* 131–143. doi:10.1080/17439760.2012.662994

Flanagan, O. (1991). *Varieties of moral personality: Ethics and psychological realism.* Cambridge, MA: Harvard University Press.

Fleeson, W. (2004). Moving personality beyond the person–situation debate: The challenge and the opportunity of within-person variability. *Current Directions in Psychological Science, 13,* 83–87. doi:10.1111/j.0963-7214.2004.00280.x

Frimer, J. A., Biesanz, J. C., Walker, L. J., & MacKinlay, C. W. (2013). Liberals and conservatives rely on common moral foundations when making moral judgments about influential people. *Journal of Personality and Social Psychology, 104,* 1040–1059. doi:10.1037/a0032277

Frimer, J. A., & Walker, L. J. (2009). Reconciling the self and morality: An empirical model of moral centrality development. *Developmental Psychology, 45,* 1669–1681. doi:10.1037/a0017418

Frimer, J. A., Walker, L. J., Dunlop, W. L., Lee, B. H., & Riches, A. (2011). The integration of agency and communion in moral personality: Evidence of enlightened self-interest. *Journal of Personality and Social Psychology, 101,* 149–163. doi:10.1037/a0023780

Frimer, J. A., Walker, L. J., Lee, B. H., Riches, A., & Dunlop, W. L. (2012). Hierarchical integration of agency and communion: A study of influential moral figures. *Journal of Personality, 80,* 1117–1145. doi:10.1111/j.1467-6494.2012.00764.x

Gilligan, C. (1982). *In a different voice: Psychological theory and women's development.* Cambridge, MA: Harvard University Press.

Haidt, J. (2008). Morality. *Perspectives on Psychological Science, 3,* 65–72. doi:10.1111/j.1745-6916.2008.00063.x

Haidt, J., & Graham, J. (2007). When morality opposes justice: Conservatives have moral intuitions that liberals may not recognize. *Social Justice Research, 20,* 98–116. doi:10.1007/s11211-007-0034-z

Hardy, S. A., Walker, L. J., Olsen, J. A., Skalski, J. E., & Basinger, J. C. (2011). Adolescent naturalistic conceptions of moral maturity. *Social Development, 20,* 562–586. doi:10.1111/j.1467-9507.2010.00590.x

Hoffman, M. L. (2000). *Empathy and moral development: Implications for caring and justice.* Cambridge, England: Cambridge University Press.

Hogan, R. (1982). A socioanalytic theory of personality. In M. M. Page (Ed.), *Nebraska Symposium on Motivation: Vol. 30. Personality: Current theory and research* (pp. 55–89). Lincoln: University of Nebraska Press.

Kohlberg, L. (1981). *Essays on moral development: Vol. 1. The philosophy of moral development*. San Francisco, CA: Harper & Row.

Magnusson, D. (2003). The person approach: Concepts, measurement models, and research strategy. In S. C. Peck & R. W. Roeser (Eds.), *New Directions for Child and Adolescent Development: No. 101. Person-centered approaches to studying development in context* (pp. 3–23). San Francisco, CA: Jossey-Bass.

Matsuba, M. K., & Walker, L. J. (2004). Extraordinary moral commitment: Young adults working for social organizations. *Journal of Personality, 72,* 413–436. doi:10.1111/j.0022-3506.2004.00267.x

Matsuba, M. K., & Walker, L. J. (2005). Young adult moral exemplars: The making of self through stories. *Journal of Research on Adolescence, 15,* 275–297. doi:10.1111/j.1532-7795.2005.00097.x

McAdams, D. P. (1995). What do we know when we know a person? *Journal of Personality, 63,* 365–396. doi:10.1111/j.1467-6494.1995.tb00500.x

McAdams, D. P. (2006). *The redemptive self: Stories Americans live by*. New York, NY: Oxford University Press.

Oliner, S. P. (2003). *Do unto others: Extraordinary acts of ordinary people*. Boulder, CO: Westview.

Paulhus, D. L., & Trapnell, P. D. (2008). Self-presentation of personality: An agency–communion framework. In O. P. John, R. W. Robins, & L. A. Pervin (Eds.), *Handbook of personality psychology* (pp. 492–517). New York, NY: Guilford Press.

Reimer, K. S. (2009). *Living L'Arche: Stories of compassion, love and disability*. London, England: Continuum.

Rokeach, M. (1973). *The nature of human values*. New York, NY: Free Press.

Schwartz, S. H., Cieciuch, J., Vecchione, M., Davidov, E., Fischer, R., Beierlein, C., . . . Konty, M. (2012). Refining the theory of basic individual values. *Journal of Personality and Social Psychology, 103,* 663–688. doi:10.1037/a0029393

Turiel, E. (1983). *The development of social knowledge: Morality and convention*. Cambridge, England: Cambridge University Press.

Walker, L. J. (in press). Moral personality, motivation, and identity. In M. Killen & J. G. Smetana (Eds.), *Handbook of moral development* (2nd ed.). New York, NY: Taylor & Francis.

Walker, L. J., & Frimer, J. A. (2007). Moral personality of brave and caring exemplars. *Journal of Personality and Social Psychology, 93,* 845–860. doi:10.1037/0022-3514.93.5.845

Walker, L. J., Frimer, J. A., & Dunlop, W. L. (2010). Varieties of moral personality: Beyond the banality of heroism. *Journal of Personality, 78,* 907–942. doi:10.1111/j.1467-6494.2010.00637.x

Walker, L. J., & Hennig, K. H. (2004). Differing conceptions of moral exemplarity: Just, brave, and caring. *Journal of Personality and Social Psychology, 86,* 629–647. doi:10.1037/0022-3514.86.4.629

Walker, L. J., & Pitts, R. C. (1998). Naturalistic conceptions of moral maturity. *Developmental Psychology, 34,* 403–419. doi:10.1037/0012-1649.34.3.403

Zimbardo, P. G. (2007). The banality of evil, the banality of heroism. In J. Brockman (Ed.), *What is your dangerous idea? Today's leading thinkers on the unthinkable* (pp. 275–276). New York, NY: Harper Perennial.

LAWRENCE J. WALKER *is a professor of psychology and the associate dean of graduate studies at the University of British Columbia.*

King, P. E., Oakes Mueller, R. A., & Furrow, J. (2013). Cultural and contextual issues in exemplar research. In M. K. Matsuba, P. E. King, & K. C. Bronk (Eds.), *Exemplar methods and research: Strategies for investigation. New Directions for Child and Adolescent Development, 142,* 41–58.

4

Cultural and Contextual Issues in Exemplar Research

Pamela Ebstyne King, Ross A. Oakes Mueller, James Furrow

Abstract

This chapter specifically addresses how exemplar methods are especially relevant to examining cultural and contextual issues. Cross-cultural, cultural, and indigenous psychologies are discussed in order to highlight how studying actual exemplars in their unique and complex developmental contexts has the potential to identify themes that either differ between or hold constant across distinct peoples and cultures. The chapter addresses basic assumptions of exemplar research and specifics of the method that are sensitive to the incorporation of cultural and contextual influences. Suggestions are made as to how exemplarity research can be even more effective to explore development in a valid means across cultures and be more attentive and applicable to local cultures. © 2013 Wiley Periodicals, Inc.

NEW DIRECTIONS FOR CHILD AND ADOLESCENT DEVELOPMENT, no. 142, Winter 2013 © Wiley Periodicals, Inc.
Published online in Wiley Online Library (wileyonlinelibrary.com). • DOI: 10.1002/cad.20048

41

One of the most acute challenges facing the field of developmental psychology today is finding means and methods of understanding how culture and context impact development (Arnett, 2008; Brown, Larson, & Saraswathi, 2002; Jensen, 2008, 2012). Although culture and context have long been recognized as seminal influences on development, currently the field's dominant methodologies emphasize nomothetic findings and universals across populations. Frequently used quantitative strategies restrict the depth and richness of investigation, and all too often do not allow for variation among diverse contexts to emerge. Exemplar methods, especially those that combine quantitative and qualitative approaches, have been demonstrated to be effective for discovering both nomothetic and idiographic findings (Bronk, King, & Matsuba, this volume; Colby & Damon, 1992; King, Clardy, & Ramos, 2013), providing opportunities for the particularities of cultural and contextual influences to be revealed. Although exemplar methods generally have been employed to investigate psychological constructs that are less understood (e.g., thriving, purpose, spirituality), this chapter addresses how exemplar strategies are especially relevant to examine cultural and contextual issues that influence development.

In order to highlight some of the potential opportunities and challenges of exemplar research, this chapter identifies some of the key challenges in the broader field of psychology that are specifically raised by the unique subfields of cross-cultural, cultural, and indigenous psychology and discusses them in light of exemplar research. Further, because personal and cultural narrative has been identified as being particularly relevant to addressing cultural issues (Shweder et al., 2006), this chapter discusses the particularly valuable role of participants' narratives. Therefore, although exemplarity research has historically employed both quantitative and qualitative methods, this chapter refers primarily to the qualitative or case study approach to exemplar research. From this perspective, we then discuss some of the guiding assumptions of qualitative exemplar strategies with regard to understanding the participant in context.

In order to illustrate how cultural approaches are relevant to exemplar methods, we present and discuss a specific study on adolescent spiritual exemplars from around the world (King et al., 2013). The sample of 30 youth, ranging from 12 to 21 years old, was geographically and culturally diverse, with six exemplars from India, six from Kenya, six from the United Kingdom, six from the United States, four from Peru, and two from Jordan. The sample contained atheist, Buddhist, Catholic, Hindu, Muslim, Protestant, Jewish, Sikh, and one self-identified mixed-religion youth.

In addition to the youth spiritual exemplars, we offer examples from other exemplar studies that illustrate both the cultural considerations illuminated by exemplar research, as well as the ways in which such research may be made relevant when applied in various settings. We then discuss existing and potential challenges to current exemplar strategies that are evident in the literature. Finally, recommendations for further investigation and understanding of cultural and contextual influences using exemplar methods are offered.

Cross-Cultural, Cultural, and Indigenous Psychologies

Given the increased awareness of global diversity and its relevance to human development and functioning, psychologists have begun to question many long-held assumptions of the field. In his prominent article in the *American Psychologist*, Arnett (2008) challenges the premise that most human science studies may generalize to all human beings regardless of their sample's nationality and culture of origin. The massive diversity of living conditions—value systems, socioeconomics, education, ethnicity, and resources—throughout the world challenges the current field's tendency to generalize across cultures and developmental contexts. Similarly, Shweder et al. (2006) posit that studies on the development of the self have generally proceeded primarily from one cultural viewpoint and draw upon a set of untested assumptions about the self. Furthermore, Jensen (2012) has challenged the broader field of developmental psychology to bridge cultural and universal approaches in order to identify theoretical and methodological frameworks that are sensitive to cultural issues, just as she has done so effectively in the moral domain (Jensen, 2008). The fields of cross-cultural psychology, cultural psychology, and indigenous psychology have arisen, in part, to address such concerns (Allwood, 2011; Chirkov, Ryan, & Sheldon, 2011; Jensen, 2008; Kim, Yang, & Hwang, 2006; Shweder et al., 2006).

While each of these fields differs in its particular approach to psychological phenomena, they all draw upon theoretical frameworks and methodologies that are sensitive to issues of particularity in developmental processes and outcomes.[1] All three fields have emerged as a response to the tendency in psychology to speak in terms of universal traits. In seeking to identify the possible cultural biases of psychological theories, *cross-cultural psychology* has historically emphasized the existence of universals, but has paid attention to assumptions and methods that enable researchers to understand how universal qualities are expressed differently across a variety of distinct settings. One example of such an approach can be found in cross-cultural positive psychology, which seeks to identify both psychological universals (e.g., well-being) and their diverse expression given culture-specific characteristics of various populations (e.g., collectivist vs. individualist goals). As such, cross-cultural psychological research design pays attention to the dialectic between universal human capacities and needs and specifically examines cultural influence on the expression and fulfillment of these needs (Chirkov et al., 2011). Nevertheless, the often controversial assumption of universal traits is foundational to this approach.

Although cross-cultural psychology represents a much-needed step forward for the field, other approaches have emphasized the shortcomings of the cross-cultural framework. Specifically, the fields of both cultural and indigenous psychology argue that researchers need to expand their understanding of cultural sensitivity beyond a search for universal tendencies and their potentially unique expressions in different cultural contexts (Cheung, van de Vijver, & Leong, 2011; Jensen, 2012; Shweder et al., 2006). They argue for a movement beyond treating cultural perspective as a form of bias, and therefore something to be eliminated from research procedures or controlled for in data analysis. Instead, their aim is to employ theory and methods that allow for cultural and contextual particularities to surface.

Thus, the question of *cultural psychology* is: How do cultural practices and mentalities shape who humans become, what they believe, and how they behave (Jensen, 2008; Shweder et al., 2006)? Cultural psychology aims to understand the psychologies of different people groups by means of culturally sensitive theories and methods. For developmental psychologists working within a cultural psychology framework, such context-specific distinctions might offer insight into the healthy development or treatment of children and adolescents from divergent contexts and cultures. From this perspective, cultural psychologists use ecologically sensitive theories and methods, and value the search for both cultural differences and cultural similarities (Jensen, 2012).

While both cultural and indigenous approaches to psychology are interested in intracultural particularities, *indigenous psychology* is unique insofar as it emerges exclusively within a specific culture and for that culture. As such, indigenous psychology is based on the philosophical assumptions and intellectual history of the specific culture. In contrast, cultural psychology often involves experts from one people group seeking a deeper understanding of the key beliefs and practices of another people group. Indigenous studies are led by local scholars and experts in the culture, and research is conducted among the indigenous population. It gives priority to the study of culturally unique psychological and behavioral phenomena or characteristics of the people. From an indigenous psychology perspective, culture is as much under scrutiny as the psychological phenomenon being studied; culture is inseparably bound up with psychological phenomenon. Thus, given that a fundamental premise of indigenous psychologies is that they are to be anchored in local culture, from an indigenous approach it is often to be expected that many unique indigenous psychologies will be developed around the globe (Poortinga, 1999).

Although cross-cultural, cultural, and indigenous psychologies all examine psychological phenomena and processes, they each have a different emphasis that stems from important philosophical assumptions and results in different methodologies. One distinguishing ontological issue is how the field's assumptions about universality guides the theories and methods used for inquiry in each approach. At the risk of oversimplifying these important fields, one could say that cross-cultural psychology examines psychological differences *between cultures*, cultural psychology emphasizes psychological diversity *within another culture*, and indigenous psychology emphasizes the exploration of psychological phenomena *by a culture*. While all are sensitive to cultural differences, each holds different implications for exemplar methods.

Exemplar Methods

Although often intended to examine an aspect of human development that is recognized across different peoples, exemplar methods allow for cultural and contextual issues to emerge in the data. Exemplar methods explicitly examine a specific construct in actual lives of individuals who exhibit it in an intense and highly developed manner. Studying the lives of exemplar participants reveals what the development of the construct looks like (Bronk, 2012). Qualitative case study exemplar methods consider youth in their unique and complex developmental contexts. In this way, exemplar methods provide a "real world" look at development of a given trait. As described in the introduction to this volume, whereas other methods, such as purely quantitative approaches, may strip away potentially "muddling" influences of experience, context, and confounding variables, the exemplar approach does not (Bronk et al., this volume). As a result of focusing on lived experience, qualitative exemplar methodologies, in particular, may provide insight into characteristics and processes related to the phenomenon under investigation that are hard to capture through other methods, allowing researchers to distinguish what is nomothetic, differential, and idiographic—and therefore potentially contextually salient. The following section addresses some of the basic assumptions of exemplar research and specifics of the method that are sensitive to the incorporation of cultural and contextual influences. At every step of the research design, cultural and contextual variation may be taken into consideration.

Participants as Experts

Consistent with the various cultural psychologies, exemplar methods take seriously the meanings and interpretations of the participants. Most qualitative exemplar methods explore lesser-understood and multifaceted domains of development by specifically engaging the exemplar-participant as a collaborator in investigation, allowing the participant to bring his or her cultural ideology and experiences to the data. This is done, in large part, through interviews designed to evoke reflection by asking exemplars to narrate, interpret, and share their opinions on particular experiences from their own lives. In doing so, such interviews enable participants to express their own interpretations of the meaning of their actions, commitments, and ideals. Indeed, when compared with standardized questionnaires, these types of in-depth, semi-structured interviews allow for "thicker" data that have the capacity to reveal the complexity of exemplars' experiences and interpretations of self and meaning (Reimer, Dueck, Adelchanow, & Muto,

2009). This aim is consistent with all three forms of cultural psychologies. Because participants are nominated for exemplifying the construct under investigation, they are viewed as "experts," and their unique stories, experiences, and interpretations are taken seriously. Their expertise in the area of study and high levels of self-awareness make their own representations and interpretations an invaluable resource in the exploration (Colby & Damon, 1992).

It is important to note that although exemplar participants are viewed as experts in the phenomenon under examination, the method promotes a dialectic between data and existing literature, and between participant and researcher. Indeed, it is critical to recognize that although the participant might be a "procedural expert" (i.e., I do something well), this does not necessarily make them a "declarative expert" (i.e., I can explain what I am doing, why I do it, and how I do it). Existing research suggests that at times what is happening with moral exemplars is implicit, procedural, automatic, and nonconscious (Haidt, 2001). Consequently, a method that allows for in-depth interaction between existing theory, participant input, and researchers' insight is critical to maximizing understanding of the expression and development of the construct under investigation.

Nomination Process

Given the expert status of the participants in exemplar methodology, selection procedures are seminal to the methodology and are an important opportunity for cultural considerations. As presented previously in this volume, exemplar methodologies use a form of nomination criteria for selection of participants. Criteria are usually developed through a systematic and rigorous process based on theory, literature, and recognized experts in the field of the domain (see Colby & Damon, 1992; Hart & Fegley, 1995; Reimer et al., 2009). Although theory or existing definitions may inform initial criteria, iterative processes are then used, in which various diverse and (hopefully) culturally informed experts revise and refine criteria in order to maximize cultural sensitivity. Bronk (2012) points out that, ideally, nomination criteria should be made as concrete as possible, being both narrow enough to be descriptive of a "highly developed" group of individuals who manifest the construct under investigation and simultaneously broad enough to capture a range of characteristics and experiences within the exemplary sample.

The issue of nomination criteria is addressed differently from cross-cultural, cultural, and indigenous psychologies. Like traditional psychology, cross-cultural positive psychology would utilize nomination criteria designed to solicit individuals who possess a potentially universal trait or who embody a potentially universal psychological phenomenon. As such, cross-cultural psychologists begin with broad criteria capable of "catching" a range of behaviors in different cultures or adjust the criteria in particular settings in order to allow for the nomination of exemplars who manifest the construct differently in different cultures. In contrast, from the perspective of cultural psychology, the criteria for nomination are initially created taking the ideology, practices, and norms of different culture(s) into account, with the intention of yielding a sample representative of the variability of the phenomenon within a culture. In both cross-cultural and cultural psychology, experts on or from the culture may have input on the nomination criteria in order to be sensitive to cultural nuances. On the other hand, in an indigenous psychology research design, the nomination criteria could be devised by local experts and based on local ideology and practices with the intent to solicit a sample that highlights the unique values and behaviors of that culture. As such, indigenous psychologists would likely be minimally concerned with creating nomination criteria that could generalize across cultures. Instead, the validity of such criteria *within* the culture becomes paramount.

The adolescent spiritual exemplar study (considered a hybrid of the cultural and cross-cultural approaches) highlights how nomination criteria may take cultural issues into consideration (King et al., 2013). For instance, the construction of nomination criteria involved social scientists, theologians, clergy, and youth practitioners from different countries and diverse spiritual traditions, who provided four iterations of feedback on the criteria. In addition, the study employed a local researcher in each country where data was collected to ensure that local religious and cultural issues were included in the nomination criteria. This iterative process was designed to minimize the potential impact of Western, American, and Christian intellectual and religious biases into the definition of exemplary spirituality.

In addition to the *content* of nomination criteria, nominators themselves also contribute to the *contextualization* of the criteria. Specifically, the use of individual nominators in exemplar research influences the interpretation of the criteria in local settings. So although criteria may be based on theory or a normative understanding of the topic, indigenous nominators interpret the criteria for themselves when making their selections of potential participants and thereby infuse the data with cultural and contextual variability. For example, in the spiritual exemplar study, most nominators identified young people who practiced a religion as an expression of their spirituality. However, one nominator from Northern Ireland nominated an atheist as a spiritual exemplar. This boy's family had experienced much violence and loss in the name of religion. The political-religious climate in which he was raised greatly impacted his experience of spirituality. The case of this boy demonstrates how researchers influence the study by their selection of the nominators, and must take into consideration the diversity of their nominators.

Typically, researchers select informed nominators, who although not scholars, are expert practitioners who have a clear understanding of how the nomination criteria are manifested in real lives in their context (see Bronk et al., this volume). By using local, lay people as nominators, investigators hope to elicit a local, context-specific interpretation of the nomination criteria, in order to increase the construct validity of the exemplar nominations in each culture being studied. The importance of nominator choice is evident in a study by Oakes Mueller, Sando, and Furrow (2010), who found that the same nomination criteria solicited significantly different "caring exemplars" when used by nominators from varying organizational contexts within the same city. Specifically, although all nominators were asked to identify adolescents who had demonstrated particular, concrete acts of caring, youth nominated through schools reported significantly different values than youth nominated through community-based organizations. Specifically, teacher-nominated exemplars reported stronger endorsement of academically oriented personal values such as conformity and achievement (Schwartz, 1996), suggesting teachers may have included academic responsibility in their understanding of "care."

Selection of nominators varies between the different cultural approaches. Cross-cultural psychologists would select individuals that understand the potential universality of the construct, but are sensitive to its potential unique manifestations in different cultures. In contrast, cultural psychologists would select nominators that are sensitive to the diversity of cultural ideologies of the sample. Such nominators would be attentive to and have intimate knowledge of the culturally specific expressions of values, beliefs, and behaviors relevant to the construct under scrutiny. In an indigenous study, *both* researchers *and* nominators would be native to the culture and have a deep understanding of the beliefs and meaning systems of the culture. It is important to note that after nominations are completed, researchers again can influence the cultural variation and depth of understanding by using practical criteria to select the final sample from the nomination pool to ensure cultural diversity. Researchers often use demographics to select a sample balanced with gender, age, income, ethnicity, religion, and other demographic variables.

For example, in the spiritual exemplar study (King et al., 2013), scholars and expert practitioners from multiple different religious and spiritual traditions were recruited as nominators. Specifically, of the 17 nominators, six countries were represented, and nine spiritual/religious traditions were represented. In addition, in order to increase the diversity of their sample and, thereby, sensitivity to within- and between-culture variations, researchers oversampled U.S. exemplars from Buddhist, Jewish, and Muslim communities.

Interview Protocol

In addition to sample selection, data collection also provides many opportunities for contextual and cultural influences. An interview itself is a cultural construct, and the format of the interview (e.g., one-to-one, collective) is a cultural concern. For example, the development of the interview protocol involves many of the same issues as the development of the nomination criteria. So from a cross-cultural or cultural psychology perspective, although often initially based on existing theory, the protocol will be refined by different cultural experts, adding probes sensitive to issues of meaning and interpretation. This will allow the protocol to either (a) reveal cultural-specific characteristics of a psychological universal (as is the intention of cross-cultural psychology) or (b) yield findings that describe the variation within a given culture (as is the aim of cultural psychology). For example, within the adolescent spiritual exemplar study, the local research consultant in India pointed out the importance of asking about spirituality in the context of the family and not just as an individual experience (King et al., 2013). Within an indigenous design, the protocol would be created expressly by locals and based on local theory, ideology, and literature so as to better reveal particularities of the culture.

Again, in order to be relevant in the different religious and cultural contexts, the protocol used in the spiritual exemplar study underwent 11 iterations of feedback from scholars and practitioners from different academic disciplines, religious traditions, and cultures (King et al., 2013). In addition, the local research coordinators reviewed and modified questions when necessary in order to elicit cultural nuances in each setting. The interview protocol was also pilot tested on subjects from various religious traditions and ages in order to give feedback regarding cultural and religious relevance. Some of the modifications of the content of the protocol included the importance of asking about a young person's sense of self-concept from their own perspective, as well as the perspective of others. Expert input also raised the issue of probes that were sensitive to potentially pertinent settings within a young person's ecology that may not be as obvious from a Western perspective, such as grandparents or even ancestors. In addition, local researchers gave guidance on appropriate behaviors and dress for interviews.

Use of Narrative

Although mixed methods are often used in exemplar research, the richest descriptions of exemplary lives typically result from semi-structured clinical interviews (Colby & Damon, 1992; Piaget, 1929). Narratives gained through interviews allow for "thick" data and unique interview experiences with enough structure to explore common themes across interviews, while simultaneously retaining enough flexibility to identify unique characteristics and experiences that highlight sources of cultural and contextual influence (see Colby & Damon, this volume; Reimer et al., 2009). Indeed, the solicitation of narrative is a methodological tool often used in cross-cultural, cultural, and indigenous approaches to data gathering. It provides a means of capturing the reality of participants' psychological lives, while allowing for the emergence of specific individual and cultural meanings and values. Specifically, Shweder et al. (2006) identify narrative as a cultural universal, and one of the most powerful interpretive tools that humans possess for organizing, interpreting, and valuing human experience and behavior. Narrative data allows researchers to distinguish between universal human capacities and needs, culture-specific characteristics or expressions of these universals, and entirely unique cultural phenomena (Chirkov et al., 2011).

In addition, interviews are generally conducted in person and administered in the participant's indigenous context, allowing for researchers to get to know participants' environments and make contextual observations about personal meanings. It is noted that the emphasis on participants' meanings and interpretations of their experiences and life are only as good as the protocol allows and the clinical skills of the interviewer. Thus, protocol development and training of the interviewer cannot be underestimated. While indigenous studies would involve local interviewers, cross-cultural and cultural psychologists might utilize culturally astute interviewers from another culture.

Although many exemplar studies are based on the assumption of the existence of universal qualities (see Walker, this volume), some studies approximate an indigenous approach. When examining a specific psychological phenomenon, indigenous researchers investigate both the specific content and the involved processes of the phenomenon. Such research begins with a thorough immersion into the natural, concrete details of the phenomenon under exploration (Kim et al., 2006). Essentially, this is the intention of exemplar strategies—for the researcher to immerse him- or herself in the life, perspectives, and opinions of the exemplar. For example, Walker and Hennig's (2004) study of Canadian heroes was an exemplar study designed by Canadians, using national Canadian awards as nomination criteria, data gathering, and analysis by Canadians (see also Walker, this volume, for further discussion).

Data Analysis

Although exemplar methods are defined more by participant selection and sample than by analysis, data analysis allows for opportunities for cultural and contextual input. Although the depth and complexity of data common among qualitative exemplar studies makes comparisons between samples challenging, common themes across exemplars may be identified. For example, three common themes of spirituality, specifically transcendence, fidelity, and action, emerged from the analysis of the adolescent spiritual exemplars (King et al., 2013).

From a cross-cultural perspective, qualitative or quantitative findings may be compared between cultures by using culture or context as a predictor variable to highlight cultural distinctions and particularities.

Nevertheless, such researchers remain vigilant to context-specific meanings in their interpretations of findings. For example, transcendence was experienced between the individual and God or Allah in Christianity and Islam, respectively. However, transcendence was more often reported to be apparent in communal experiences among family members or faith community for the Jewish and Hindu youth.

From a cultural psychology perspective, analysis would include culturally relevant predictor variables that differ *within* the local population, so as to uncover the diversity of the expression of a psychological phenomenon within a culture (Shweder et al., 2006). Within indigenous psychology, analysis would be conducted by locals who are familiar with the meanings of the culture; ideally, empirical findings would be distributed and reviewed by different members of the culture to ensure that the various meanings and interpretations of the culture were accounted for in the data gathering and analysis. Although not a purely indigenous design, findings from the spiritual exemplar study illustrate this point. From a Western positive youth development perspective, we anticipated volunteer service as relevant to youth spirituality; however, cultural norms greatly informed how spirituality was enacted in different contexts. Specifically, in more industrialized contexts, exemplars described engaging in service to the poor. For example, American and British exemplars often participated in "mission" trips to developing nations where they assisted locals in various ways. In less industrialized contexts, however, the exemplars served through leading worship or teaching younger children within their mosque or church (King et al., 2013).

In summary, the complex and arduous methods that comprise exemplar research—especially qualitative exemplar research—allow for complex data that may facilitate the identification of themes that either differ between or hold constant across distinct peoples and cultures. Whether the investigator is more concerned with commonalities or particularities, exemplar research may be adapted to maximize the inclusion of culture and context. The findings are usually descriptive in nature, and may both highlight cultural issues and generate hypotheses to be further tested or explored in more diverse or specific samples.

Future Directions

Although, for the most part, existing exemplar studies have focused primarily on highly developed psychological characteristics, and to a lesser extent culture, exemplar methods are well poised to explore development in a valid means across cultures and be more attentive and applicable to local cultures. Even so, some modifications of typical exemplar strategies could significantly enhance the cross-cultural sensitivity and applicability of their findings. An interdisciplinary approach that considers the perspectives of cross-cultural, cultural, and/or indigenous psychologies gives specific direction for deliberate cultural and contextual inquiry. Indeed, while some studies are explicitly designed to explore and examine cultural issues (King et al., 2013; Reimer et al., 2009), the identification of culture-specific expressions is secondary, at best. The following discussion addresses specific methodological recommendations for exemplarity research of both types, with an aim to increasing their sensitivity to issues of culture and context.

Exemplar researchers will better understand developmental-cultural issues when methods allow for the consideration of an individual's reciprocal interactions with his or her environment. Currently, qualitative exemplar methods consider the lives of actual individuals in the complexity of their developmental contexts. In-depth inquiry naturally facilitates developmental psychologists' aim at revealing the "person-context" interaction (Lerner, 2006), the "dialectical synthesis" (Valsiner, 2011), or "transactional events" (Rogoff, 1990). Narratives, as well as other potential qualitative or quantitative sources of data, illuminate the complexities of the bidirectional influences between the developing person and their peers, families, culture, faith, and so forth. Not only do qualitative exemplar methods allow for social and macrocultural issues to be considered, but they also allow for historical trends relevant to exemplarity to be included in analysis (see Colby & Damon, 1992, this volume). Furthermore, given the "thick" narrative data common to exemplarity research, these methods allow for the emergence in analysis of less familiar systems of development than those typically assumed by dominating Western theories.

In addition, exemplar methods maximize their understanding of developmental-cultural issues when methods include the analysis of developmental trajectories across the lifespan. The field of developmental psychology would benefit from exemplarity research that not only focuses on the characteristics or nature of a psychological phenomenon (e.g., spirituality, thriving), but also on the different developmental trajectories across and within cultures that lead to them. In other words, research is needed that not only reveals *what* is embodied in these exemplary lives, but also *how* it came to be the case. For example, researchers might ask: What influences in childhood and adolescence occurred, and how do such influences differentially affect exemplars from different contexts? Or what culture-specific personal experiences shaped their ability to exemplify the quality?

The inclusion of different-aged exemplars and/or longitudinal data would enable researchers to better answer such questions. Specifically, Jensen (2012) suggested that analyzing the developmental trajectories of different cultures affords a window into the relative influences of nature and (cultural) nurture. She posits that children often represent a clearer test for universality, whereas adults represent a cleaner examination of cultural diversity. Specifically, because adults have had longer to become acculturated to the values and narratives of their community, they serve as a more adequate representation of larger cultural norms of their community. In contrast, because of their youth and their station in life, children are more malleable and less culturally socialized. Because of this, future exemplar studies would benefit from conducting parallel analyses of child, adolescent, adult, and later-life exemplars, as well as longitudinal exemplar studies. Both within and across cultures, such analyses could help to differentiate idiosyncratic qualities of individual exemplars *both* from universal qualities of exemplars *and* from culture-specific particularities and developmental achievements.

A further area for improvement involves the explicit acknowledgment of researchers' guiding assumptions regarding the "goods" being exemplified in their participants. Specifically, because the focus of exemplarity research is on highly developed qualities or "end states," the method raises teleological issues. All exemplar studies involve culturally circumscribed assumptions about exemplarity. For example, Walker and Hennig's (2004) study of bravery, courage, and compassion of national heroes in Canada studied a Canadian conception of *hero*. Bronk's (2008) study of youth purpose exemplars explored a sense of purpose in youth in the United States. King et al.'s (2013) study on youth spiritual exemplars attempted to study the commonalities and differences of youth in different cultures and faith traditions. However, each of these studies operated under different cultural teleological assumptions. Exemplar methods naturally allow for the acknowledgment of the role of culture in this way. In particular, the creation of nomination criteria and nomination procedures assume culturally preferred end states. Consequently, exemplar researchers must be explicit about their nomination strategies and recognize the cultural and contextual assumptions on which their studies are based. Do researchers take a normative or folk understanding of the construct under investigation (e.g., Maclean, Walker, & Matsuba, 2004; Reimer et al., 2009), in which lay people are assumed to be experts in nomination criteria? Or do they take an expert-scholar approach to identifying nomination guidelines (e.g., Colby & Damon, 1992; King et al., 2013)? Such assumptions must be explicitly stated so as to avoid either conflating such perspectives or unwittingly imposing one's own teleology on a culture.

Although the current literature calls for attention to less-Western psychological constructs such as interdependence (Jensen, 2012), it is important to remain open to different cultures' developmental teleology—a culture's goals for development. Given that most existing developmental research is based on Western theories and their often-implicit assumptions regarding goals for human development, the field of developmental psychology would benefit from future studies that explicitly focus on exploring different cultures' goals for development through careful and rigorous exemplar methods. Exemplar researchers need to be clear of their goals and aware of the cultural teleology they are examining.

No doubt, culture and context matter. Indeed, Oakes Mueller et al.'s (2010) finding that, despite the use of standardized nomination criteria, "care exemplars" nominated by teachers appeared to possess traits of "academic exemplars" should serve as a cautionary lesson. Such findings remind future researchers to heed the challenges of identifying effective nomination criteria, assessing the appropriateness and influence of the context in which nominations occur, and considering such complexities in their analysis and interpretation of findings. Specifically, while exemplar studies may inform observations of what is and speculation as to what may be, such findings do not necessarily offer a final validation of the specific "universal qualities" being investigated. Indeed, this is a point of cultural and indigenous psychologies, that although a certain characteristic may be manifested within a certain set of exemplars, we cannot know how common or prevalent these characteristics are among others without *both* investigating those from other contexts *and* importing particular teleological and epistemological assumptions.

In addition, Oakes Mueller et al. (2010) also raised the potential confounding issue of the "halo effect" (Thorndike, 1920), whereby an individual who is viewed favorably on one dimension may be viewed favorably on other dimensions. For example, the Oakes Mueller et al. (2010) finding that teachers nominated achievement-oriented students as "caring exemplars" raises the question of whether the expression of a high-value behavior in the school context led teachers to perceive academic performers as caring youth as well. Further exemplar research must consider the extent to which context may influence the way in which nominators understand and apply specific evaluative terms.

In addition to being aware of the potential influence of context, scholars using an exemplar strategy have much to gain from being intentional about their specific approaches to considering culture and context in their studies (see also discussion of dispositional and situational issues by Walker, in Chapter 3 of this volume). As discussed in this chapter, cross-cultural, cultural, and indigenous psychologies have very specific theoretical and methodological approaches that are consistent with their unique understanding of culture. In many ways, exemplar research is well poised to help bridge the exploration of commonalities and particularities in developmental psychology. Because exemplar studies focus on a highly developed psychological construct, there is the possibility for relevance to different people groups (Colby & Damon, this volume), but issues of generalizability need to be explicitly addressed in light of culture and ecological validity. In addition, the descriptive nature of qualitative exemplar findings also allows for culturally unique expressions or culturally ideographic findings to be acknowledged (Cheung et al., 2011). Future studies would benefit from clearly stating as research goals whether the primary intention is to study commonalities and/or particularities, describing how their methods account for culture, pointing toward potential commonalities and differences across participants, and discussing the inevitable limitations regarding issues of generalizability across cultures.

New Directions for Child and Adolescent Development • DOI: 10.1002/cad

Although exemplar methods provide an effective means of bridging universal and cultural approaches (Jensen, 2012), further improvements can be made so as to increase an understanding of cultural developmental issues. Specifically, studies that balance the tyranny of universals with an obsession with fragmentation will facilitate an understanding of psychological phenomena that illuminate different trajectories in different contexts. Although the field is currently short on indigenous approaches and would gain from a deeper and more nuanced understanding of non-Western cultures, the greatest benefit will come when indigenous or culture-centered studies are effectively translated to other settings and cultures. Specifically, by developing an indigenous psychological framework that uses the native language and meaning systems of a culture to speak authentically to that culture, the corresponding danger is that the conclusions of such studies become relatively inaccessible to those from other cultures. Although it is helpful to document and describe ideographic particularities, theoretical and methodological frameworks that can include them in the larger scientific dialogue will benefit our current understanding and care of children and youth.

For example, the procedures taken in the adolescent spiritual exemplars study (King et al., 2013) represent an attempt at such first steps in collaborating among different cultures. To be sure, the study was still led predominantly by Western researchers, and therefore likely carries with it the biases of this perspective. Nevertheless, the researchers in this study attempted to partner at almost every level of investigation (nomination criteria, protocol development, ethical guidelines, data collection, and analysis), so as to minimize such bias and maximize the study's sensitivity to culture-specific narratives, values, and meaning systems. Future exemplar studies might also benefit from utilizing native leaders as creators of and collaborators in the research process. In short, with the exception of indigenous studies that aim primarily to collect culture-specific data, future exemplar studies would benefit from expanding and innovating the methods for collaboration across cultures.

Furthermore, just as the field of literature benefits from translations and compendia of literary works, indigenous exemplar studies may benefit from discussions or commentaries that aim to use the languages of other fields (e.g., anthropology) to help situate their native findings within their larger cultural narratives and meaning systems. Indeed, the field as a whole might benefit from the qualitative equivalent of meta-analyses, wide-ranging commentaries on multiple exemplar studies that aim both to contextualize the findings of each study within its native culture, and to identify across studies various culture-specific expressions of more universal phenomenon. Of course, such analyses must walk a narrow line. Just as indigenous exemplar studies risk missing the universals in human development, any failure to attend to the uniqueness of exemplars in different cultures risks mistaking real *qualitative* differences between cultures for

NEW DIRECTIONS FOR CHILD AND ADOLESCENT DEVELOPMENT • DOI: 10.1002/cad

quantitative differences in *apparently universal* (and typically Western) psychological constructs. By walking this line, such analyses may allow the findings of one indigenous study to serve as *hypothesis generators* for cross-cultural studies, even while respecting indigenous psychology's cautious refusal to simply use their own populations to *test the hypotheses* of other cultures' psychologies.

In summary, future exemplar studies will benefit from increased collaboration between researchers and local indigenous leaders, a greater effort *both* to contextualize findings *and* to generalize across studies, and the nomination and study of exemplars at multiple developmental levels from within the same culture. Such shifts have the potential to maximize the native strength of exemplar research to identify both universal and culturally particular qualities and behaviors associated with a given construct.

Conclusion

Although, for the most part, current exemplar studies share the traditional "universalistic aspirations" (Jensen, 2012) of the greater field of developmental psychology and have aimed to elucidate less understood domains of human development, exemplar strategies are well positioned to illumine both common and particular expressions of human development. The method's focus on exemplarity allows for the exploration of cultural ideals, potentially revealing psychological constructs that Western-centric theories and methods may overlook. In addition, rigorous nomination procedures, data gathering, and analysis allow for universal and cultural investigation. Exemplar strategies yield rich descriptions of remarkable lives of individuals who embody a construct under examination with consistency and intensity. Although exemplar methods are designed to point to common characteristics and processes associated with the construct of interest, qualitative methods can prevent these commonalities from being stripped of the context and culture from which they emerge. As such, exemplar studies highlight idiographic findings and pay special attention to individual variance, allowing for the role of culture and content to be evident. In this way, the study of exemplarity provides the opportunity to study the diversity of what is deemed exceptional and noble in different cultural contexts, which nevertheless serves to inspire a sense of common humanity.

References

Allwood, C. M. (2011). On the foundation of the indigenous psychologies. *Social Epistemology, 25*, 3–14.

Arnett, J. J. (2008). The neglected 95%: Why American psychology needs to become less American. *American Psychologist, 63*(7), 602–614.

Bronk, K. C. (2008). Humility among adolescent purpose exemplars. *Journal of Research on Character Education, 6*(1), 35–51.

Bronk, K. C. (2012). *The exemplar methodology: An approach to studying the leading edge of development.* Manuscript under review.

Brown, B. B., Larson, R. W., & Saraswathi, T. S. (2002). *The world's youth: Adolescence in eight regions of the globe.* New York, NY: Cambridge University Press.

Cheung, F. M., van de Vijver, F. R., & Leong, F. L. (2011). Toward a new approach to the study of personality in culture. *American Psychologist, 66*(7), 593–603.

Chirkov, V. I., Ryan, R. M., & Sheldon, K. M. (Eds.). (2011). *Human autonomy in cross-cultural contexts.* Dordrecht, Netherlands: Springer.

Colby, A., & Damon, W. (1992). *Some do care: Contemporary lives of moral commitment.* New York, NY: The Free Press.

Haidt, J. (2001). The emotional dog and its rational tail: A social intuitionist approach to moral judgment. *Psychological Review, 108*(4), 814–834.

Hart, D., & Fegley, S. (1995). Altruism and caring in adolescence: Relations to moral judgment and self-understanding. *Child Development, 66,* 1346–1359.

Jensen, L. A. (2008). Coming of age in a multicultural world: Globalization and adolescent cultural identity formation. In D. L. Browning (Ed.), *Adolescent identities: A collection of readings* (pp. 3–17). New York, NY: The Analytic Press/Taylor & Francis Group.

Jensen, L. A. (2012). Bridging universal and cultural perspectives: A vision for developmental psychology in a global world. *Child Development Perspectives, 6*(1), 98–104.

Kim, U., Yang, K., & Hwang, K. (2006). *Indigenous and cultural psychology: Understanding people in context.* New York, NY: Springer Science + Business Media.

King, P. E., Clardy, C. E., & Ramos, J. S. (2013). Adolescent spiritual exemplars: Exploring spirituality in the lives of diverse youth. *Journal of Adolescent Research.* doi:10.1177/0743558413502534

Lerner, R. M. (2006). Developmental science, developmental systems, and contemporary theories of human development. In R. M. Lerner & W. Damon (Eds.), *Handbook of child psychology: Theoretical models of human development* (6th ed., Vol. 1, pp. 1–17). Hoboken, NJ: Wiley.

Maclean, A., Walker, L. J., & Matsuba, M. (2004). Transcendence and the moral self: Identity integration, religion, and moral life. *Journal for the Scientific Study of Religion, 43*(3), 429–437.

Oakes Mueller, R. A., Sando, L., & Furrow, J. L. (2010, March). *Contextual influences on exemplar nominations: Value differences between teacher- and community leader-nominated moral exemplars.* Paper presented at the biannual meeting of the Society for Research in Adolescence, Philadelphia, PA.

Piaget, J. J. (1929). *The child's conception of the world.* Oxford, England: Harcourt, Brace.

Poortinga, Y. H. (1999). Do differences in behaviour imply a need for different psychologies? *Applied Psychology: An International Review, 48*(4), 419–432.

Reimer, K. S., Dueck, A. C., Adelchanow, L. V., & Muto, J. D. (2009). Developing spiritual identity: Retrospective accounts from Muslim, Jewish, and Christian exemplars. In M. Souza, L. J. Francis, J. O'Higgins-Norman, & D. Scott (Eds.), *International handbook of education for spirituality, care and wellbeing* (pp. 507–523). Amsterdam: Springer Netherlands. doi:10.1007/978-1-4020-9018-9_28

Rogoff, B. (1990). *Apprenticeship in thinking: Cognitive development in social context.* New York, NY: Oxford University Press.

Schwartz, S. H. (1996). Value priorities and behavior: Applying a theory of integrated value systems. In C. Seligman, J. M. Olson, & M. P. Zanna (Eds.), *The psychology of values: The Ontario symposium, 8* (pp. 1–24). Hillsdale, NJ: Lawrence Erlbaum.

Shweder, R. A., Goodnow, J. J., Hatano, G., LeVine, R. A., Markus, H. R., & Miller, P. J. (2006). The cultural psychology of development: One mind, many mentalities. In R. M. Lerner & W. Damon (Eds.), *Handbook of child psychology: Theoretical models of human development* (6th ed., Vol. 1, pp. 716–792). Hoboken, NJ: Wiley.

Thorndike, E. L. (1920). A constant error in psychological ratings. *Journal of Applied Psychology, 4*(1), 25–29.

Valsiner, J. (2011). The development of individual purposes: Creating actuality through novelty. In L. Jensen (Ed.), *Bridging cultural and developmental approaches to psychology: New syntheses in theory, research, and policy* (pp. 212–232). New York, NY: Oxford University Press.

Walker, L. J., & Hennig, K. H. (2004). Differing conceptions of moral exemplarity: Just, brave, and caring. *Journal of Personality and Social Psychology, 86*(4), 629–647.

Note

1. Although a full discussion of the complexity and interrelatedness of these fields is beyond the scope of this chapter, distinctions between cross-cultural, cultural, and indigenous psychologies evident in the literature are generalized in order to illuminate the nuances of culturally oriented approaches.

Pamela Ebstyne King *is an associate professor of marital and family studies with the Thrive Center for Human Development in the School of Psychology at Fuller Theological Seminary, Pasadena, California.*

Ross A. Oakes Mueller *is an associate professor of psychology at Point Loma Nazarene University, San Diego, California.*

James Furrow *is Evelyn and Frank Freed Professor of Marital and Family Therapy in the School of Psychology at Fuller Theological Seminary, Pasadena, California.*

New Directions for Child and Adolescent Development • DOI: 10.1002/cad

Matsuba, M. K., & Pratt, M. W. (2013). The making of an environmental activist: A developmental psychological perspective. In M. K. Matsuba, P. E. King, & K. C. Bronk (Eds.), *Exemplar methods and research: Strategies for investigation. New Directions for Child and Adolescent Development, 142,* 59–74.

5

The Making of an Environmental Activist: A Developmental Psychological Perspective

M. Kyle Matsuba, Michael W. Pratt

Abstract

This chapter reviews the research on environmental exemplars, or activists. General themes that have been identified in the literature include early experiences in nature, the influence of other people and organizations, opportunities for environmental education, environmental self and identity formation, and generativity. With these themes in hand, we construct a developmental model suggesting a possible trajectory toward environmental activism. We also discuss possible implications of these findings with reference to the current state of our planet and what may be done to reverse current trends. © 2013 Wiley Periodicals, Inc.

The State of Our World

Our planet is in trouble. Over the past century, the human population has more than quadrupled, the use of water and energy has increased 9-fold and 16-fold, respectively, CO_2 emissions have increased 17-fold, hypoxic marine "dead zones" are ever expanding, and our food, water, and soil contain thousands of industrial contaminants (Rees, 2008). In the face of these startling facts and dire warnings, the continued calls for action by the international community have been made over and over again (United Nations, 2012). Yet these calls have gone unheeded: Little improvement has been seen in the health of our planet (Scientific American, 2010). For Canadian academic and environmentalist icon David Suzuki, this fact is a clear indication of the failure of the environmental movement to significantly change people's worldview about, and their behavior toward, the environment (David Suzuki Foundation, 2012). To effect significant behavioral changes requires a fundamental paradigm shift in how humans see and act in their environment. Yet how is this shift to happen?

To answer this question, we have turned to research on environmental activists to gain insight. Like other areas of exemplarity research (Bronk, King, & Matsuba, this volume; Damon & Colby, this volume; King, Oakes Mueller, & Furrow, this volume; Walker, this volume), we believe that the study of committed environmental activists can help us to better understand the processes and pathways leading to positive environmental behaviors among us all. In this chapter, we review the growing literature on environmental activists and identify the common themes emerging from this literature, particularly focusing on early childhood and adolescent experiences. We also review and expand on those papers that have proposed developmental models to explain the pathways toward environmental identity and action.

Environmental Activists

Who are environmental activists? According to researchers, environmental activists have included people who were involved in the leadership of environmental organizations, environment-related education, land management and preservation, environmental design, ecology, and other environmental activities involving the law, lobbying, and writing (Horwitz, 1994). Environmental activists have also been identified based on their active participation in a range of environmental issues, including recycling and waste management, pollution and radiation, transportation, land use planning, and habitat and wildlife preservation (Chawla, 1999). Finally, environmental activists have been chosen for study based on their occupations or graduate work in areas such as entomology, mycology, herpetology, and ornithology (James, Bixler, & Vadala, 2010). Thus, there is great diversity in the

NEW DIRECTIONS FOR CHILD AND ADOLESCENT DEVELOPMENT • DOI: 10.1002/cad

kinds of work in which "environmental activists" engage, and in the environmental philosophies that motivate their work.

While the kinds of work that environmental activists do and the underlying environmental philosophies that motivate their work vary widely, few studies have considered whether there are meaningful differences between the various kinds of activists. Rather, the majority of studies have tended to look for commonalities across environmentalist types. Consequently, we focus on these commonalities, acknowledging that further research is needed to study within-group variability.

Environmental Ethics

Just as there are many types of environmental activists, so too are there many reasons that can motivate activism. In some cases, activists are motivated out of their obligation to environmental ethical principles. For example, some environmental activists may adopt an "anthropocentric" perspective by assigning intrinsic value predominantly to human beings. From this perspective, environmental issues are important considerations in as much as they relate to the welfare of human beings. Hence, nonhuman creatures and things in nature are viewed as only of instrumental value to human life. Other environmental activists may adopt a "biocentric" perspective and see nature as having its own intrinsic value, and thus as having certain inherent rights (Leopold, 1949), although articulating what those rights are and their limits has proven controversial (e.g., Moore & Nelson, 2010). A more extreme biocentric form, the deep ecology movement, calls for biospheric egalitarianism (Naess, 1973). This movement considers all living things as having intrinsic value; hence, we are morally obligated to take care of all living organisms.

While the literature on environmental ethics continues to expand, little work has been done to empirically understand the environmental ethics behind activists' engagement. The one exception to this is Horwitz's work (1996), in which she asked 29 prominent American environmental activists from two east coast states to describe their environmental ethics. She reported that most activists saw themselves in close relation to and interdependent with nature. Many talked about their respect or reverence for nature, and thus their moral obligation to protect it. Implicit within their responses was the intrinsic value they placed on nature. Moreover, having an environmental ethic obligated people to act in ways that respected nature through acts of caring for it or by preventing its harm. Thus, these environmental activists appeared to be acting largely from a biocentric perspective. Interestingly, it is this shift from an anthropocentric to a biocentric view of nature that Suzuki calls for if there is any hope of saving our planet (David Suzuki Foundation, 2012). But how do we cultivate this shift in perspective among the wider population?

Common Themes From Research on Environmental Activists

In this section, we highlight some of the emerging themes revealed through studies on environmental activists that suggest how such a shift in perspective could occur. These themes include early and sustained social and educational experiences in nature, environmental self and identity formation, and the personality quality of generativity.

Experiences in Nature. The sociocultural context in which we are raised and the experiences that emerge within that context shape who we are as individuals. This seems true with regard to each of our perspectives toward the environment. Anthropologist Wade Davis (2007) writes: "A child raised to believe that a mountain is the abode of a protective spirit will be a profoundly different human being from a youth brought up to believe that a mountain is an inert mass of rock ready to be mined" (p. 65). As this quote illustrates, our sociocultural upbringing and experiences dramatically shape the developmental trajectory of individuals. This seems to be apparent based on findings from qualitative studies on environmental activists. A prevalent theme emerging from research on environmental activists is their experiences with nature. These experiences in the unspoiled natural world are perceived by environmental activists as important factors in their development of an environmental ethic of care (Horwitz, 1994, 1996). Horwitz (1996) also reported that experiences in nature often triggered a positive affective response with activists mentioning feelings of "joy" in, "love" of, or "awe" of nature, with the latter suggesting that these experiences can have a spiritual quality.

Typically, these positive experiences in nature were recalled by activists as occurring early in their lives as a result of their participation in recreational activities such as playing in nature or through living in a rural context (Horwitz, 1996). Most environmental activists spoke of these early experiences as foundational in the development of their relationship with the environment. For instance, Chawla (1999) interviewed environmentalists from Kentucky and from Norway about their environmental efforts and the sources of their commitment. Her environmentalists reported that these early experiences interacting with nature created the first "bond" with the natural world that then became part of the activist's "regular rhythm of daily life" (Chawla, 1999, p. 19). In fact, early positive experiences in nature were a consistent finding in most studies on environmental activists, and have frequently been interpreted as being pivotal in shaping the life trajectories of activism (e.g., Chan, 2009; Horwitz, 1996). Further, in college and community samples of adults surveyed, Mayer and Frantz (2004) found connection to nature predicted self-reported ecological behaviors, such as turning off the lights when vacating a room, and a sense of subjective well-being.

Recent quantitative empirical research supports the importance of positive childhood experiences in retrospect. In a general sample of adults, Wells

NEW DIRECTIONS FOR CHILD AND ADOLESCENT DEVELOPMENT • DOI: 10.1002/cad

and Lekies (2006) found positive correlations between self-reported child-hood participation in nature (e.g., hiking; camping; hunting; picking flowers, fruits, and vegetables) and later adult attitudes and behaviors toward the environment. In addition, in our own recent research, we found that activists versus comparison nonactivist individuals reported significantly more positive experiences with nature in their early life narrative accounts (Bisson, Alisat, Norris, & Pratt, 2012). Below is a quote from one of our young adult environmental activists:

> I'm from up north, so we go on a canoe trip every year, and the environment, well, not the environment, but the river and everything, it's so nice, and it's clean and that's important. I guess what happened would be canoeing down the river with my dad and some of his friends. I guess canoe down the river. [*What were you thinking?*] I was really young most of the time, I was probably about six to twelve, we used to do it every year, but I guess how nice it was, that's what I'd be thinking. I guess I was feeling happy. An impact would just be … I have an attachment to canoeing and stuff like that, just because it was part of my childhood. I guess what it would say about who I am is that I like the outdoors.

Yet positive experiences in nature were not the only motivational factor that seemed to contribute toward activism. Many environmental activists also mentioned negative experiences involving harm of nature as influential. Witnessing the destruction of valued places through clear-cutting of forested areas or the damage done to nature through pollution or radiation have been identified as influential experiences in the lives of environmental activists both in America and in Norway (Chawla, 1999). The influence of experiences of environmental harm on environmental actions may be mediated through their challenge to one's environmental ethics. Horwitz (1996) reported that her activists mentioned similar early childhood and adult experiences involving environmental destruction as influences on their developing environmental sensitivity. Finally, in our research, we found that negative experiences with nature were linked to both a stronger environmental identity and a stronger sense of connection with nature for activists as well as nonactivists (Bisson et al., 2012). Together, this body of research suggests that the reporting of these experiences in nature, both positive and negative, has been identified by environmental activists to be important in the construction of their attitudes and beliefs about the environment and in their movement toward environmental activism.

People, Organizations, and Society. Typically, early experiences in nature are not solitary experiences. Rather, these early experiences that activists mentioned involve other people, particularly family members and peers (Chawla, 1999). Often, exposure to nature occurred in the context of trips with their families that involved hiking, canoeing, and so on (Horwitz, 1996). In these cases, people were reported as being important in providing the opportunity to access nature. Participation in environmental or outdoor organizations, such as Boy Scouts or Girl Scouts, Youth Conserva-tion Corps, and other outdoor clubs, also figured prominently in the lives of environmental activists (Chawla, 1999; Horwitz, 1996). This was evident in our own work (Alisat, Norris, Pratt, Matsuba, & McAdams, 2013), as illustrated in the quote below from one of our young adult environmental activists:

> I've always absolutely loved nature and environment and trees, gardens and things that grow and plants and animals, whatever, and I like being outside, and I'd done some volunteer work, for the hatchery before that for a few years. It was just small things really, trying to help out. But I hadn't really been aware of, or plugged into all the big problems, and the community of people trying to do things. So it was really joining the "Student Environment Center" that really triggered me to, to get plugged in. And it's pretty small steps but just, you get involved in the Sierra Club, whatever, and from there, the amount of things that have happened over the last four or five years, have kind of taken off and bloomed.

Environmental Education. Activists' interest in environmental issues was often piqued through direct and indirect experiences with nature, both positive and negative, that were frequently social in nature. These social interactions provided a context for the exchange of information. That is, parents and adults belonging to various environment-related organizations played important roles in providing children with knowledge about nature. Chawla (1999) reported that much of her activists' early education about nature was gained through significant others, membership in organizations, and school programs. And with this newfound knowledge about nature, activists were better able to deepen their skill sets with regard to interacting with nature (Horwitz, 1996).

In adolescence and early adulthood, formal education through high school and college classes was mentioned by some activists as being in-fluential in the shaping of their environmental activism (Horwitz, 1996). However, formal education was often not what triggered an interest in en-vironmentalism, but rather provided the opportunity for activists to delve deeper into environmental issues, or to help uncover the breadth of issues associated with environmentalism (Horwitz, 1996). Thus, environmental education, both formal and informal, was often reported as significant in nurturing the "seeds" of environmentalism planted earlier in life and in shaping people's later environmental attitudes and behaviors.

Environmental Self and Identity. Further, these sustained experi-ences in nature seem to shape environmental activists' identities. Hor-witz (1996) found that environmental activists reported a strong bond or identification with nature. According to Horwitz, a developing sense of self as being intimately connected to the environment was part of the process in the formation of an environmental ethic. Similarly, Chan (2009), through her life narrative interviews with leaders in the environmental sustainability movement, found that they mentioned having a unique and special connection to nature early in their life stories. Together these findings suggest that the formation of an environmental self seemed to begin to emerge in childhood for many activists.

As activists transitioned into adolescence and emerging adulthood, the importance of the environmental self to their identities became evident. In our study, we compared young adult environmental activists to a group of individuals, matched on age, gender, and community, on a variety of measures (Matsuba et al., 2012). We found that environmental activists scored higher on measures of general identity maturity and, most notably, of specific environmental identity. In James et al.'s (2010) study, they reported that their environmental professionals developed an awareness of their own environmental identities in adolescence and emerging adulthood as they made decisions regarding the career paths they would follow. In fact, James et al. described "crystallization" moments in their activists' career pursuits when they became fully aware of their fascination with nature and of their own competence and confidence in their knowledge and skills regarding the environment. Hence, sustained involvement with nature and in environmental organizations was reported to have shaped how activists perceived themselves and the identities to which they committed themselves as they emerged into adulthood.

Generativity. Finally, research suggests that generativity is an important motivational factor in environmental activism. *Generativity* refers to people's concern and care for the next generations. In the context of our work, generativity refers to people's concern and care for the environment and how its current state may impact future generations. Horwitz (1996) identified generativity as a salient theme in her study of environmental activists, as reflected in concerns for the future of our world's ecosystems. Chan (2009) also identified generativity as a driving force behind her environmental activists' commitment toward sustainability. In our work, we found our environmental activists to score higher on measures of generativity relative to comparison individuals (Matsuba et al., 2012). Further, we found that generativity was a mediating factor between identity development and environmentalism: With identity maturation and commitment came growing concerns for the next generation (generativity), which in turn led to further engagement in environmental activities.

A Developmental Model of Environmental Activism

From reviewing the literature on environmental activists, an emerging story seems to be unfolding regarding the developmental trajectory of environmental activism. While caution is necessary in proposing such an account, given the retrospective nature of the data on environmental activists and the potential bias in reporting past events, we nevertheless speculate about possible model pathways leading toward engagement in environmental causes—speculations that will require future research support. To help us in this endeavor, we draw upon research from developmental, moral, and religious/spiritual psychology, believing that these areas can help us understand the formative processes involved in the development of environmental activists. We also draw upon the psychological literature investigating the relationship between children and nature (e.g., Kahn & Kellert, 2002). Based on these bodies of work, there are two related clusters of findings on which we will focus: early childhood experiences in nature, and the environmental self and identity formation in adolescence.

Childhood Experiences in Nature. Recent attempts at explaining environmental activism include early exposure to the environment as a critical developmental influence (Chawla, 2007; James et al., 2010; Wells & Lekies, 2006). This early exposure to nature may be facilitated by two factors. First, our human genetic heritage may predispose people to prefer the natural environment versus other built urban environments (Balling & Falk, 1982; Kahn, 2002; Weinstein, Przybylski, & Ryan, 2009; Wilson, 1984). According to Wilson's biophilia hypothesis, humans have a genetically based propensity to affiliate with other living organisms and with certain features of our environment of evolutionary adaptation that were typical of our species' earlier history (e.g., a special enjoyment of savannahs, forests, waterways). Such a hypothesis has been proposed to explain research findings that have demonstrated people's general preferences for, and the health benefits associated with being in, certain aspects of nature (Howell, Dopko, Passmore, & Buro, 2011). Second, as mentioned, early exposure to nature is likely to be socially facilitated through family outings, or through participation in community organizational or school-related activities. Horwitz (1996) suggested that such exposure may foster an esthetic appreciation of nature and provide early knowledge acquisition about nature. Together, the predisposition to be close to nature and the opportunity to be in nature were the early life realities for many of us. Yet few of us have become environmental activists. Why?

Perhaps one important factor is the role of sustained exposure to nature throughout childhood and adolescence. James et al. (2010) argued that early experiences in nature lead to more formal activities in nature (i.e., organization-based outdoor recreational programs), and that these formal activities facilitate the development of environmental competencies (e.g., camping and survival skills). Such developing environmental knowledge and skills may help to expand children's interest to be in nature. Finally, Chawla (2007) emphasized the interactive cycle between children and their environment. As children freely explore their environments, their experiences leave lasting, positive impressions that encourage further engagement with nature. This is because nature can provide novel challenges that maintain and build children's interest. In addition, experiences in nature can serve to expand children's environmental knowledge and competencies and facilitate their more general cognitive and affective development (Kellert, 2002). Hence, it is this continual, sustained exposure to and interaction with nature that may be important in contributing to environmental activism.

Work within developmental psychology suggests possible underlying mechanisms to explain children's movement toward or away from environmentalism. According to social cognitive theories, children develop cognitive schemas about their world and cognitive scripts to guide them in how to act in that world, which are influenced by context (Crick & Dodge, 1994; Dubow, Huesmann, & Boxer, 2009). Within the context of nature, therefore, social cognitive theorists would argue that early experiences in nature are foundational because they facilitate the development of children's cognitive schemas and scripts focused on nature and the natural environment. For example, aggressive children growing up in poor neighborhoods may have acquired cognitive schemas that depict the world as hostile, and have adopted normative attitudes and beliefs that aggression is an acceptable behavioral response in situations (Guerra, Huesmann, & Spindler, 2003). As we know, children living in poverty are at particular risk for negative outcomes, including higher levels of aggression (Evans, 2004; Leventhal & Brooks-Gunn, 2000). Some have attributed the cause of aggression, in part, to increased exposure to violence on the streets and in the home. Witnessing such violence facilitates the development of cognitive schemas and scripts focused on violence and aggression (Dubow et al., 2009).

Within the context of nature, then, social cognitive theorists would argue that early experiences in nature are foundational because they facilitate the development of children's cognitive schemas and scripts focused on nature and the natural environment. Further, positive experiences in nature may lead to a sense of closeness to nature, which may then motivate further engagement (Weinstein et al., 2009). Over time, these sustained experiences in nature will shape children's cognitive schemas about their world, their scripts on how to interact in that world, and the life stories they craft that feature prominently the environmental episodes of their past.

Likewise, a failure to expose children to natural environments can have negative longer-term consequences, such as a fear of the wilderness or the disgust experienced by witnessing nature in action (e.g., a decaying dead animal). Such emotions may work to prevent children from exploring nature later in life. Bixler and Floyd (1997) found that rural and suburban youth who scored high in disgust related to nature, and in worries and fears about the natural environment, were more likely to prefer manicured park settings and urban environments, and showed a dislike for wildland environments, compared to those who scored low on these negative emotional measures. Hence, a failure to expose children to wild nature can have negative consequences in terms of their attitudinal, emotional, and behavioral responses to nature later in life.

More recent work by Kahn, Saunders, Severson, Myers, and Gill (2008) suggest that children as young as 6 years old can be fearful of nature and still care for nature. In their study, they asked children attending an interactive exhibit on bats at a zoo about their fear of, the care for, and the rights afforded to bats. They found that while some children feared bats, this did not prevent them from caring for bats. Most children also accorded bats feelings and thoughts and certain (animal) rights. Whether these results generalized to other animals in less captive environments remains to be seen.

Sadly, most measures show the health of our planet in a state of decline, and there is very little optimism that significant environmental improvements are going to happen anytime soon. If we take the United States, the world's largest economy, as our example, there is good reason to be concerned. With the current economic downturn, the U.S. government is cutting the budgets of many of its branches, including the Environmental Protection Agency (Johnson, 2011) and the Division of Forest Services, which manages our national parks (National Parks Advocates, 2011). And the large majority of Americans continue to live in urban over rural areas (79% vs. 21%) (U.S. Department of Transportation, 2000). Given these trends in the United States, it would appear that fewer people are having, or are interested in having, wilderness experiences in nature. Yet, if early and sustained experiences in nature are critical in the development of later environmental attitudes and behaviors, as most research on environmental activists suggests, then we should be concerned that current and future generations are having fewer opportunities to experience nature.

Further, there continue to be generational shifts in our understanding of "nature." Kahn (2002) refers to this as environmental generational amnesia: "With each ensuing generation, the amount of environmental degradation increases, but each generation in its youth takes that degraded condition as the nondegraded condition—as the normal experience" (p. 106). As environmental degradation increases, and access to pristine nature diminishes, people's conceptions of nature and their closeness to nature may devolve more toward urban parks and zoos, rather than to national parks and wildlands. Similarly, Louv (2008) writes anecdotally of a "nature deficit disorder" (not a formal clinical disorder), referring to a number of behavioral problems he has observed among American children ostensibly as a result of them spending less time in the outdoors, and more time watching "screens" such as TV, computers, gaming platforms, and handheld devices. The cause of children spending less time in nature, Louv speculates, is due to parental fears of the outdoors along with less access to nature. These conditions that Kahn and Louv describe are illustrative of a growing concern by many regarding the effects that fewer experiences in wilderness are having on children's general well-being, as well as their attitudes and behaviors toward nature.

Finally, lack of access to nature may affect children's folk biology development. Coley, Solomon, and Shafto (2002) have shown that American urban children's early understanding of plants and animals is quite anthropocentric. That is, these children understand other living things in reference to human beings. This understanding is likely to be exacerbated by children's shows that anthropomorphize animals, such as Disney movies (e.g., *Finding Nemo*). Such a phenomenon is in contrast to first nations children, who are raised in indigenous communities where they have significant everyday experiences with plants and animals. These children show no early anthropocentric folk biology reasoning, but rather reason based on the similarity among all living things (Coley et al., 2002). Hence, the early folk biology development of children is not universally anthropocentric, but varies across different populations. Urban American children with few opportunities to interact in nature are more likely to have a skewed perspective of nature, including wildlife, which may impact how they interact with and respect nature later in life.

In summary, early and continued experiences in nature throughout childhood seem likely to be important in creating sustained interest and motivations to care for nature. Continual experiences with nature may be important in the creation of cognitive schemas of a natural world as children develop, and a cognitive script of how to interact in nature so that these wild places become familiar, positive spaces. Moreover, these experiences in nature are likely to be important in influencing people's attitudes toward the natural world and facilitating the development of environmental ethical principles. Finally, early and continual experiences in nature may help to contribute to aspects of cognitive development and the development of an environmental self and identity, which we turn to now.

Self, Identity, and the Environment in Adolescence. Recent work on self development suggests possible pathways to an environmental self and identity. By the age of 2 years, a sense of self is believed to exist, as captured in the well-known rouge-mirror task studies (Lewis & Brooks-Gunn, 1979) when children respond appropriately to their reflections in mirrors. From here, children begin to develop their self-concept, or mental representation of self, based on information collected on the self through experiences of sensation and reflections (Kihlstrom, Beer, & Klein, 2003). Such development is accelerated by the self's widening social interactions in relationships and groups. In its adult-like form, a self-concept is thought to be made up of a collection of multiple, context-dependent self-aspects, which are nodes that are laid out in a connectionist-type memory network (McConnell, 2011). Self-aspects include relationships, roles, and social identities (e.g., son, boyfriend, and football player). Self-aspects can also include behavioral situations or episodes (e.g., self at a party) and affective states (e.g., being angry). Each self-aspect is associated with one or more personal attributes, which include personality and affective traits, behaviors, physical characteristics, and social categories (e.g., African American male).

Further, McLean, Pasupathi, and Pals (2007) explain how self stories in childhood can play an important role in self development. They persuasively argue that with the emergence of situated stories (i.e., personal memories that are created within specific situations) comes the development of life stories and one's self-concept in childhood. For instance, the situated self stories in childhood can help shape self development, as these stories are integrated into one's broader, emerging life story in adolescence and emerging adulthood (McAdams, 2011). Events that are told repeatedly are more likely to contain personal meaning, and thus have greater impact on the developing life story. Moreover, continual specific behavioral experiences, or the situated self stories they facilitate, may begin to be abstracted out and become people's trait-like sense of the "me" (McAdams, 2011). Those important to the self become part of an individual's self-aspects and attributes (McConnell, 2011). For example, youth who continually experience and reflect on episodes involving the self engaged in caring and compassionate life events may begin to abstract out the self-attribute of caring, or of empathy (Soucie, Lawford, & Pratt, 2012).

Among environmental activists, positive and negative childhood stories about the environment may be the situated stories in their developing life narrative, and contribute to abstracting out "environmentalist" as an important self-aspect. Evidence consistent with this perspective comes from Alisat et al. (2013). Based on five situated environmental stories, these authors found that environmental activists had more developed environmental identities relative to comparison individuals. That is, environmental activists' stories (a general scene, an early scene, a moral courage story, a story where moral courage was not shown, and a turning point) were scored higher in meaning, vividness, and impact compared to non-activists' stories. These cumulative self-narrative scores also were significantly correlated with standard questionnaire measures of environmental identity across the two groups. Thus, narratives can be an important indicator of the expertise and investment of the self into an environmental identity.

Over time and continual experiences in and reflections on self and the natural environment, the environmentalist self-aspect may thus become an important part of one's sense of self. Again, James et al. (2010) write about the formation of environmental identity as being a "crystallization process" among their environmental activists. Similarly, in research on moral exemplars, Colby and Damon (1992) write about the unity of the self and morality among their interviewees. Finally, King, Ramos, and Clardy (2012), in the context of spiritual development, write about a transcendent experience when a spiritual exemplar shifts focus away from the self-as-individual to the self in relation to some "other."

If the environmental self and identity formation process is important in the development of an environmental activist, and identity formation is believed to occur in adolescence and emerging adulthood (Erikson, 1968), there are some troubling findings with regard to this current generation of youth. If we return to the United States as our case study, this contemporary cohort of youth are the least concerned about the environment, compared to youth from other cohorts spanning the last 30 years, and are assigning greater responsibility for the environment to the government (Twenge, Campbell, & Freeman, 2012; Wray-Lake, Flanagan, & Osgood, 2010). Add to this the fact that adolescence is generally considered a "time-out" period in which youth are more disengaged from nature compared to other developmental periods (Kaplan & Kaplan, 2002). Part of the reason for youths' disengagement is due to their preference to spend time with their peers, and that most typical activities they do with their peers do not involve nature. Thus, if the goal is to attract youth to the natural environment, simply providing individual opportunities to be engaged with nature will not suffice. Opportunities to interact with nature will need to be social, where individuals can interact with their peers and experience mutual support and stimulation, something we already know about when it comes to political engagement in youth and its impact on longer term social activism (see McAdam, 1990).

In summary, the environmental self and identity begin to develop in early childhood and continue to be elaborated in adolescence and into adulthood. Opportunities to engage in the natural environment allow children to develop a schema of their world as involving the natural environment, a self-schema of themselves interacting in that environment, and an emerging sense of the importance of nature to the self and its associated life story, all leading to the development of an environmental identity in seriously committed individuals. Unfortunately, recent trends in countries like the United States suggest that opportunities to form an exemplary environmental self and identity over childhood and adolescence may be diminishing.

Conclusion

Our world is in trouble. If the health of our planet is going to improve, a paradigm shift is needed in how individuals think about and act in the environment. By looking to studies on environmental activists and their autobiographical sense of self, we have gleaned insight into some factors that may be important in moving society forward to making this shift. Early and sustained experiences in natural environments that are socially facilitated are believed to be critical factors in constructing the self and worlds of activists in which the natural environment features so prominently. These situated and sustained experiences in nature are likely to be important in the development of people's environmental identities as they pass through adolescence into emerging adulthood, and narrate this journey as part of their life story. Further developmental work is needed to verify the veracity of this proposed pathway toward environmentalism, and to understand how this environmental self may sustain care and concern for the planet we all share.

References

Alisat, S., Norris, J. E., Pratt, M. W., Matsuba, M. K., & McAdams, D. P. (2013). *Caring for the future of the earth.* Manuscript submitted for publication.

Balling, J. D., & Falk, J. H. (1982). Development of visual preference for natural environments. *Environment & Behavior, 14,* 5–28.

Bisson, E., Alisat, S., Norris, J. E., & Pratt, M. W. (2012, October). *Families and nature.* Paper presented at the meeting of the Society for the Study of Emerging Adulthood, Providence, RI.

Bixler, R. D., & Floyd, M. F. (1997). Nature is scary, disgusting, and uncomfortable. *Environment and Behavior, 29,* 443–467.

Chan, T. S. (2009). *Environmental sustainability as a generative concern.* (Unpublished doctoral dissertation). Northwestern University, Evanston, IL.

Chawla, L. (1999). Life paths into effective environmental action. *Journal of Environmental Education, 31,* 15–26.

Chawla, L. (2007). Childhood experiences associated with care for the natural world. *Children, Youth and Environments, 17,* 144–170.

Colby, A., & Damon, W. (1992). *Some do care: Contemporary lives of moral commitment.* New York, NY: Free Press.

Coley, J. D., Solomon, G. E., & Shafto, P. (2002). The development of folkbiology. In P. H. Kahn & S. R. Kellert (Eds.), *Children and nature: Psychological, sociocultural, and evolutionary investigations* (pp. 65–92). Cambridge, MA: MIT Press.

Crick, N. R., & Dodge, K. A. (1994). A review and reformulation for social information-processing mechanisms in children's social adjustment. *Psychological Bulletin, 115,* 74–101.

David Suzuki Foundation. (2012, May 3). The fundamental failure of environmentalism [Web log post]. Retrieved July 19, 2012, from http://www.davidsuzuki.org/blogs/science-matters/2012/05/the-fundamental-failure-of-environmentalism

Davis, W. (2007). *Light at the edge of the world: A journey through the realm of vanishing cultures.* Vancouver, BC, Canada: Douglas & McIntyre.

Dubow, E. F., Huesmann, L. R., & Boxer, P. (2009). A social-cognitive-ecological framework for understanding the impact of exposure to persistent ethnic-political violence on children's psychosocial adjustment. *Clinical Child and Family Psychological Review, 12,* 113–126.

Erikson, E. H. (1968). *Identity: Youth and crisis.* New York, NY: Norton.

Evans, G. W. (2004). The environment of childhood poverty. *American Psychologist, 59,* 77–92.

Guerra, N. G., Huesmann, L. R., & Spindler, A. (2003). Community violence exposure, social cognition, and aggression among urban elementary school children. *Child Development, 74,* 1561–1576.

Horwitz, W. A. (1994). Characteristics of environmental ethics. *Ethics & Behavior, 4,* 345–367.

Horwitz, W. A. (1996). Developmental origins of environmental ethics: The life experiences of activists. *Ethics & Behavior, 61,* 29–54.

Howell, A. J., Dopko, R. L., Passmore, H., & Buro, K. (2011). Nature connectedness: Associations with well-being and mindfulness. *Personality and Individual Differences, 51,* 166–171.

James, J. J., Bixler, R. D., & Vadala, C. E. (2010). From play in nature, to recreation then vocation. *Children, Youth and Environments, 20,* 231–256.

Johnson, N. B. (2011, July 13). Spending bill deals steep budget cuts to EPA, Interior. *Federal Times.* Retrieved July 19, 2012, from http://www.federaltimes.com/article/20110713/AGENCY01/107130305/Spending-bill-deals-steep-budget-cuts-EPA-Interior

Kahn, J. P. (2002). Children's affiliations with nature. In J. P. Kahn & S. R. Kellert (Eds.), *Children and nature: Psychological, sociocultural, and evolutionary investigations* (pp. 93–116). Cambridge, MA: MIT Press.

Kahn, P. H., & Kellert, S. R. (Eds.). (2002). *Children and nature: Psychological, sociocultural, and evolutionary investigations.* Cambridge, MA: MIT Press.

Kahn, P. H., Saunders, C. D., Severson, R. L., Myers, O. E., & Gill, B. T. (2008). Moral and fearful affiliations with the animal world: Children's conceptions of bats. *Anthrozoos, 21,* 375–386.

Kaplan, R., & Kaplan, S. (2002). Adolescents and the natural environment: A time out? In P. H. Kahn & S. R. Kellert (Eds.), *Children and nature: Psychological, sociocultural, and evolutionary investigations* (pp. 227–258). Cambridge, MA: MIT Press.

Kellert, S. R. (2002). Experiencing nature. In P. H. Kahn & S. R. Kellert (Eds.), *Children and nature: Psychological, sociocultural, and evolutionary investigations* (pp. 115–151). Cambridge, MA: MIT Press.

Kihlstrom, J. F., Beer, J. S., & Klein, S. B. (2003). Self and identity as memory. In M. R. Leary & J. P. Tangney (Eds.), *Handbook of self and identity* (pp. 68–90). New York, NY: Guilford.

King, P. E., Ramos, J. S., & Clardy, C. E. (2012). *Adolescent spiritual exemplars: Exploring spirituality in the lives of diverse youth.* Manuscript under review.

Leopold, A. (1949). *A sand county almanac.* Oxford, England: Oxford University Press.

Leventhal, T., & Brooks-Gunn, J. (2000). The neighborhoods they live in: The effects of neighborhood residence on child and adolescent outcomes. *Psychological Bulletin, 126,* 309–337.

Lewis, M., & Brooks-Gunn, J. (1979). *Social cognition and the acquisition of self.* New York, NY: Plenum Press.

Louv, R. (2008). *Last child in the woods.* Chapel Hill, NC: Algonquin Books.

Matsuba, M. K., Pratt, M. W., Norris, J. E., Mohle, E., Alisat, S., & McAdams, D. P. (2012). Environmentalism as a context for expressing identity and generativity. *Journal of Personality, 80,* 1091–1115.

Mayer, F. S., & Frantz, C. M. (2004). The connectedness to nature scale. *Journal of Environmental Psychology, 24,* 503–515.

McAdam, D. (1990). *Freedom summer.* New York, NY: Oxford University Press.

McAdams, D. P. (2011). Narrative identity. In S. Schwartz, K. Luyckx, & V. Vignoles (Eds.), *Handbook of identity theory and research* (pp. 99–116). New York, NY: Springer.

McConnell, A. R. (2011). The multiple self-aspects framework. *Personality and Social Psychology Review, 15,* 3–27.

McLean, K. C., Pasupathi, M., & Pals, J. L. (2007). Selves creating stories creating selves. *Personality and Social Psychological Review, 11,* 262–278.

Moore, K. D., & Nelson, M. P. (Eds.). (2010). *Moral ground: Ethical action for a planet in peril.* San Antonio, TX: Trinity University Press.

Naess, A. (1973). The shallow and deep, long-range ecology movement. *Inquiry, 16,* 151–155.

National Parks Advocates. (2011, March 28). Congress slashes $101 million from National Park Service budget. More to come? *National Parks Traveler.* Retrieved July 19, 2012, from http://www.nationalparkstraveler.com/2011/03/congress-slashes-101-million-national-park-service-budget-more-come7858

Rees, W. E. (2008). *Let's get serious about (un)sustainability (Or is it already too late?).* Prince George, BC, Canada: Natural Resources and Environmental Studies Institute, University of Northern British Columbia.

Scientific American. (2010, April 21). State of the planet: A snapshot. *Scientific American.* Retrieved July 19, 2012, from http://www.scientificamerican.com/article.cfm?id=earth-day-slideshow

Soucie, K. M., Lawford, H., & Pratt, M. W. (2012). Personal stories of empathy in adolescence and emerging adulthood. *Merrill-Palmer Quarterly, 58,* 141–158.

Twenge, J. M., Campbell, W. K., & Freeman, E. C. (2012). Generational difference in young adults' life goals, concern for others, and civic orientation, 1966–2009. *Journal of Personality and Social Psychology, 102,* 1045–1062.

United Nations. (2012). *Rio+20: The future we want.* Retrieved July 19, 2012, from http://www.un.org/en/sustainablefuture

U.S. Department of Transportation. (2000). *Census 2000 population statistics: U.S. population living in urban vs. rural areas.* Retrieved July 19, 2012, from http://www.fhwa.dot.gov/planning/census_issues/archives/metropolitan_planning/cps2k.cfm

Weinstein, N., Przybylski, A. K., & Ryan, R. M. (2009). Can nature make us more caring? *Personality and Social Psychology Bulletin, 35,* 1315–1329.

Wells, N. M., & Lekies, K. S. (2006). Nature and the life course. *Children, Youth and Environments, 16,* 1–24.

Wilson, E. O. (1984). *Biophilia: The human bond with other species.* Cambridge, MA: Harvard University Press.

Wray-Lake, L., Flanagan, C. A., & Osgood, D. W. (2010). Examining trends in adolescent environmental attitudes, beliefs, and behaviors across three decades. *Environment and Behavior, 42,* 61–85.

M. KYLE MATSUBA *is a psychology instructor at Kwantlen Polytechnic University in Vancouver, BC, Canada.*

MICHAEL W. PRATT *is a professor of psychology at Wilfrid Laurier University.*

New Directions for Child and Adolescent Development • DOI: 10.1002/cad

Hart, D. A., Murzyn, T., & Archibald, L. (2013). Informative and inspirational contributions of exemplar studies. In M. K. Matsuba, P. E. King, & K. C. Bronk (Eds.), *Exemplar methods and research: Strategies for investigation*. New Directions for Child and Adolescent Development, 142, 75–84.

6

Informative and Inspirational Contributions of Exemplar Studies

Daniel A. Hart, Theresa Murzyn, Lisa Archibald

Abstract

The authors of this volume showcase the unique insights that can be gained from examining the lives of exemplars. For example, as individuals who stand out for living reflective, ethical lives, exemplars can reveal the human capacity to behave in exceptional ways despite most people's tendency to not exhibit these behaviors. The authors also discuss various advantages of the exemplar approach relative to the typical methods employed by social science. Using a person-centered approach, for instance, enables researchers of exemplar studies to delve more deeply into the details and dynamics of an individual's thought processes and behaviors. Through the combined efforts of the authors, this volume illuminates the potential learning opportunities from studying exemplars, provides accounts of lives that can inspire readers, and suggests potential paths for readers' own spiritual and moral fulfillment. © 2013 Wiley Periodicals, Inc.

Informative and Inspirational Contributions of Exemplar Studies

Exemplars, by definition, are not ordinary people. They stand out from others through action, thought, emotion, motivation, or some combination of these elements. In doing so, they elicit reflection among those interested in the human condition about the value of and influences on distinctive human lives. One goal of this volume is to showcase the unique insights that can be gained from examining the lives of exemplars. The authors of this volume advance this goal by discussing the advantages of the exemplar approach relative to the typical methods of social science. The volume's second goal is to convey how exemplars (at least those studied by the authors) succeeded in living reflective, ethical lives. The blending of these two goals has resulted in a volume that illuminates the potential learning opportunities from studying exemplars, provides accounts of lives that can inspire readers, and suggests potential paths for readers' own spiritual and moral fulfillment.

The Scholarly Landscape of Exemplar Studies

The chapters in this volume all share an approach to research. Methods of data collection, analyses of the data that are collected, and the kinds of psychological processes identified through the research are strikingly similar in the various projects that are described in the volume. In the sections that follow, we comment on the common research elements in order to highlight the strengths and weaknesses of the approach.

The Particularity of Lives and Generality of Theories. The contributions to this volume have a psychological perspective, as most authors are psychologists and therefore frequently refer to psychological constructs and theories. The series of which this volume is a member is likewise targeted to social scientists who, for the most part, are familiar with the outlines, if not the details, of psychological inquiry. Yet, despite the match in paradigmatic orientations between authors and audience, many readers will be struck by the affinity of the research outlined in the chapters with scholarship outside the social sciences, such as that found in various branches of religion, history, and literature. Colby and Damon's (Chapter 2) exegesis of critical transitions in the lives of historical moral exemplars is one example. There are many passages in their chapter that are indistinguishable in style and approach from biographies one might read of the famous individuals (Mandela, Roosevelt) they describe. This likeness raises the question of the unique contribution of exemplar studies relative to other investigations that seek to highlight the nature and origins of distinctive human lives.

A partial answer to the question can be inferred from the goals inherent to studying individual lives. Biographers elevate the details of an individual life (Donald, 1987, for an account of Thomas Wolfe) or a set of lives (Lewis, 1991, for biography of William and Henry James). Biographers clearly believe that the explorations of individual lives have implications for understanding historical periods, social phenomena, and human psychology—there's no shortage of biographers among political pundits and public intellectuals—but these implications are often relatively specific to a time and place and cannot be synthesized into general statements about anything or anyone beyond the subject(s) of the biography. Exemplar research as presented in this volume has a different slant; the analyses are weighted toward contributing to psychological theories and are little concerned with elements of lives that are independent of that purpose.

Psychobiography would seem to be a close cousin to the study of exemplars. Both approaches aim to explicitly synthesize psychological theories with the details of individual lives. Traditionally, however, psychobiography has aimed to illuminate the motivations, thoughts, and actions of a person through the application of established psychological theory (Howe & Courage, 1997). For example, there were many attempts by biographers in the 20th century to account for behavior through the application of Freudian theory. These efforts, for the most part, were intended to expand an understanding of individuals through the application of established psychological theory. Most of the chapters in this volume seek to reverse the direction of influence in the hope that studying remarkable people can invigorate theory and understanding of psychological phenomena.

The exemplar method as discussed throughout this volume shares with biography and psychobiography a focus on a small number of individuals. Yet, the concept of exemplarity by itself need not restrict investigators to exploration of the psychology of only a handful of people. Cattell (1903) aimed to study the 1000 most eminent men of history, and having identified them from biographical dictionaries of the time, attempted to statistically analyze characteristics of these great men. Terman (1926) identified 1000 school children who had high IQ scores and hoped to understand the origins and consequences of genius through analyses of this large sample. According to Cattell's and Terman's views of their samples, the most eminent men of world history and children with the capacity for genius are presumably sets of exemplars worthy of study.

Yet the works in this volume, which collectively circumscribe the exemplar approach, are methodologically inconsistent with those of Cattell and Terman, though all are concerned with remarkable lives. The exemplar approach as it emerges in this volume is characterized by an attentiveness to the details of participants' lives that cannot be applied to large samples.

In their contributing chapter, Matsuba and Pratt (Chapter 5) align the origins of environmental activism with configurations of activity (hiking and canoeing), social relationships (families), and phases of life (childhood and adolescence). The inferred relationship between these factors, based on intuitions of the investigators arising from the inspection of materials from the lives of a modest number of environmental activists, seems unlikely to have been determined from cross-tabulations of characteristics from samples as large as those used by Cattell and Terman.

The exemplar approach is also viewed by many of the contributing authors as an opportunity to apply a person-centered methodology to psychological investigation (see Hart, Atkins, Fegley, Robins, & Tracy [2003], for a recent discussion of person-centered investigations). Walker (Chapter 3), for example, has suggested that by examining closely a small number of lives, it is possible to discern the operation of psychological processes within individuals: "[T]he person-level approach examines the phenomenologically real interaction among variables within the person, which is more revelatory of functional psychological dynamics" (p. 29).

We believe the chapters in this volume reveal that exemplar research bears considerable resemblance to biography and psychobiography. For example, the exemplar approach shares a concern for details of real lives and individuals' experiences; highlights the intersections of persons with relationships, contexts, and time periods; and forwards the belief that analyzing a small number of individuals can reveal the interplay of emotions, thoughts, and actions. Yet, exemplar research differs from biography and psychobiography by aspiring to integrate psychological knowledge (not usually the goal of biography) and identify new information about how the mind works (relatively uncharacteristic of psychobiography).

History and Exemplarity. Why now? One explanation for why this volume is timely is that the exemplar approach has attracted a group of talented researchers whose work has matured sufficiently to highlight the benefits of this kind of investigation. Readers of this volume surely have reached this conclusion themselves. Most of the work in this volume, for instance, has connections to Colby and Damon's study of moral exemplars as reported in their book *Some Do Care* (1992). The rapid expansion of the exemplar approach since Colby and Damon's publication to studying new categories of exemplars, including historical figures (Colby & Damon, Chapter 2), national heroes (Walker, Chapter 3), and environmental activists (Matsuba & Pratt, Chapter 5) suggests an excitement about the value of the approach that is likely of considerable interest to the social science community.

But the exemplar research paradigm is itself part of a broad cultural trend in North America of focusing on moral and ethical exemplars. One way to reveal cultural trends is to examine books published over the past century in the United States. Google has digitized more than 5 million books that were selected for inclusion in a database based on the high quality of digitized data and the presence of metadata such as location and year of publication (Michel et al., 2011). These data are publicly available and can be downloaded from http://books.google.com/ngrams/datasets

Examining these data for the *co-occurrence* of words in phrases can indicate the extent to which ideas represented by these words are linked in the popular culture as presented in the corpus. (The evidence for this

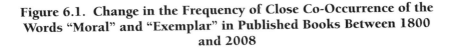

Figure 6.1. Change in the Frequency of Close Co-Occurrence of the Words "Moral" and "Exemplar" in Published Books Between 1800 and 2008

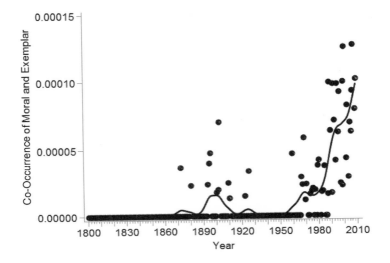

claim is explored more thoroughly in Hart & Sulik, in press.) For example, the words *war* and *nation* co-occur more often in books published in the United States in years during and immediately following the world wars. (Readers can verify this hypothesis and test others at this website: http://books.google.com/ngrams) This pattern presumably occurs because the hardships and concerns of Americans resulting from warfare during those years led them to tightly link notions of war and nation.

We used the Google corpus to explore the co-occurrence of the words *moral* and *exemplar* for each year between 1800 and 2008. Dummy codes (0 = absent; 1 = present) for the word *moral* and for the word *exemplar* were created. We cross-tabulated these dummy codes and calculated the Jaccard proximity score. This measure excludes from the calculation any similarity phrases in which both moral and exemplar were absent, thus avoiding the inflation of the measure of association. This procedure provides an estimation of the semantic connection of *moral* with *exemplar* for each year in the two-century span. The results are presented in Figure 6.1.

Two trends are evident in the figure. The first is that *moral* and *exemplar* were rarely linked in the 1800s in American books, a situation that changed for about 20 years at the juncture of the 19th and 20th centuries. Second, and most importantly for our purposes here, the last 40 years have witnessed a substantial increase in the co-occurrence—the confluence of meaning—of moral and exemplar. Note that the sharp increase in the link between *moral* and *exemplar* among U.S. publications began long in advance of Colby and Damon's (1992) seminal social science contribution about moral exemplars, and was well underway before Susan Wolf's (1982) oft-cited philosophical exploration of moral saints, a notion similar to the idea of moral exemplars.

It appears, then, that the fascination with the exemplar method as a means to explore ethical life can be viewed as one facet of a cultural trend occurring in the United States in the last quarter of the 20th century. Ethical life in full bloom—whether moral or spiritual—in our current times is judged to be (a) remarkable and (b) the product of the actions, thoughts, emotions, and motivations of unusual people (exemplars). Charles Taylor (1993) observed that modernity brought a pronounced division between private and public spheres of life and a growing belief that ordinary activities within the private sphere were imbued with considerable moral significance: family responsibilities, career responsibilities, and so on. The rising fascination with ethical exemplars over the years, as suggested by Figure 6.1, may signal an increasing appreciation for lives lived in the public sphere, which require efforts to align personal thought and action with culturally negotiated norms and ideals. In other words, exemplars may be a growing popular interest in American culture not only because they are "more ethical," but perhaps also because they exhibit forms of ethical life that modernity's ascension has made unusual.

Indeed, most of the authors in this volume view exemplars as revealing forms of ethical life not typically observed. For example, Walker reveals how self-regarding motivations can spur moral exemplars to ethical actions. More specifically, Matsuba and Pratt detail a biocentric perspective, which they interpret as obliging environmental exemplars to both recognize the intrinsic value of nature and protect its resources.

Methods, Mechanisms, and Insights

The chapters in the volume all share an approach to research. Methods of data collection, analyses of the data that are collected, and the kinds of psychological processes identified through the research are strikingly similar in the various projects that are described in the volume. In the sections that follow, we comment on the common research elements in order to highlight the strengths and weaknesses of the approach.

Personal Narratives. Most of the chapters in this volume rely heavily on interviews with exemplars to understand their lives. One reason for this approach is that exemplars as subjects of study are identified once they have exhibited extraordinary ethical behaviors. The authors of this volume further infer that exemplars reached their status through an extended developmental process. Exemplars' memories of childhood and adolescence therefore facilitate understanding of the course of transformations that culminate in exemplarity. For example, Matsuba and Pratt discuss how early life experiences in nature, such as canoeing, have been found across studies of environmental exemplars to profoundly influence individuals toward lives of activism.

Those who study autobiographical memory find that ordinary adults' recall of their own personality change is influenced by their theories of aging. These theories may consequently predispose adults to recall greater change in their own personalities than suggested by longitudinal assessments of their personalities across adulthood (Ross, 1989). Developmental processes reconstructed from interviewing exemplars may thus emphasize change and transformation more than is warranted. Though this is an important concern, none of the contributing authors in our view assumes that exemplars are capable of bias-free recall of events long past. In other words, distortions that characterize autobiographical memory are at least implicitly recognized in the analyses conducted in each of the chapters.

The prominence of personal accounts in this volume elicited through interviews is also driven by the respect the contributing researchers have for the reflective, synthetic abilities of the exemplars they study. None of the exemplars' personal accounts posits a genetic or biological advantage that channels them to their fates; nor do any of the accounts suggest that early-formed personality or cognitive traits—the kinds of stable dispositions represented by the five-factor model of personality, or IQ, for example—place individuals on railroad tracks destined to exemplarity. Instead, each chapter showcases insightful individuals reflecting on their lifelong experiences that have continuously steered them toward ethical goals.

Biographers would likely criticize the authors for the relative lack of other kinds of source materials (e.g., interviews with parents, inspection of personal documents, and so on). Psychologists who value methods that reduce the interpretative influences of both the persons under study and the investigators who study them would be similarly concerned with the centrality of personal narratives in investigations featured throughout the volume. However, several of the present authors likewise note the need for other kinds of studies less reliant on narratives and interpretations to buttress the findings reported here. Walker, calling for more objective methodologies to substantiate exemplars' self-reports, relays findings from several comparison group studies that have assessed the differential characteristics between caring and bravery exemplars and their respective groups of nonexemplar counterparts. Certainly using different methods to compare new samples of exemplars against ordinary folks can deepen our trust in the findings that are reported throughout the volume. That said, the present authors' views of exemplars as reflective, thoughtful people who craft remarkable lives justify the research program outlines they present throughout the volume.

Mechanisms. Many social scientists will be drawn toward agreement with the authors' inferences by the evidence presented for exemplars' synthetic, reflective capacities. Yet, many of the same social scientists will find considerable dissonance between the accounts offered throughout the volume and the kinds of explanatory mechanisms regnant in psychology today.

Throughout the present volume, authors have identified limitations to the experimental approaches most common in current psychology scholarship. Colby and Damon, for example, find issue with experimental morality studies that focus on a normative sample's average response to an ethical situation without including examples of exemplary individuals' capacities for differing responses. They warn that, unlike conclusions gained from studies that account for the responses of moral exemplars, "inferences based on the limits of typical responses will lead to a distorted view of morality" (Colby and Damon, p. 17). Walker likewise critiques experimental research for studying "contrived" behaviors in manipulated test settings rather than authentic actions taken by individuals in the social world (Walker, p. 28).

These criticisms seem well-founded. Yet, the kinds of ethical life accounts outlined throughout this volume differ from experimental approaches not only in the extraordinary nature of their participants, but also in the level of causal mechanisms that are allowed. For example, the trolley experiments that Colby and Damon identify in Chapter 2 are limited for understanding moral life in just the ways Colby and Damon claim, yet the trolley experiments' focus on moral judgments made in fractions of a second allows for precise manipulation of cues and alignment with momentary brain states. There is unfortunately an enormous gap between our understandings of what occurs moment to moment in moral life (trolley experiments) and the kinds of explanatory concepts invoked to understand ethical exemplars. Whether the insights gained at the granular level of rapid moral judgments can be synthesized with the mechanisms identified through the study of exemplars remains to be determined. Nonetheless, the task of integrating these bodies of knowledge seems important. As the authors in this volume point out, for example, researchers interested in moral and spiritual psychology can benefit from the insights presented through exemplar accounts in the chapters. However, we believe that benefits can flow in the other direction as well; the extension of well-studied psychological mechanisms can animate portraits of remarkable people collected by exemplar researchers. This kind of informational integration is unlikely to be fully achieved, yet the efforts to bridge study areas will, we believe, lead to new insights.

Insights.   Each chapter offers a glimpse of a new perspective on ethical life that, when taken together, can inform researchers about the potential circumstances and psychological processes involved in pursuing an ethical lifestyle. For example, Matsuba and Pratt discuss in Chapter 5 the internalization of the environmentalist identity that takes shape when an interest in the environment develops into a passion for devoting one's professional career to the environment's protection. Matsuba and Pratt share the accounts of many environmental exemplars who can recall the turning point at which they noted that their interest in the environment had to be accompanied by career skills that would enable them to work toward environmental preservation.

In Chapter 3, Walker illustrates how exemplars are able to integrate agentic and communal motives to move them to ethical action. According to studies by Walker and colleagues examining the nature of this integration, moral exemplars sought communal goals as ends in themselves, as well as agentic goals to help meet those communal ends. In other words, moral exemplars demonstrate self-interest to the extent that such self-interest aligns with and forwards their other-directed, or communal, interests.

Finally, King, Oakes Mueller, and Furrow explain in Chapter 4 how exemplarity development takes place within very "unique and complex developmental contexts" (p. 45). Developmental psychology can thus benefit from exemplar research for its ability to highlight the influence of cultural contexts on the development of various constructs, including exemplary traits. Considering developmental psychology's tendency toward universalist frameworks, King et al. argue that developmental researchers should explicitly consider culture as an important independent variable when determining the factors influencing development. Meanwhile, developmental and cultural psychologists should continue to use qualitative techniques that feature the detailed accounts of particular events, contexts, and youth perception of experiences. Recognizing the differences that become apparent between such accounts is beneficial when trying to gain a complex, cross-cultural understanding of influences on exemplarity development.

Inspiration

Although not an explicit goal of this volume, the accounts of exemplars provided herein incite inspiration. The Latin roots of *inspiration* connote being filled by, to inflame, and to breathe in (Hart, 1998). Similarly, in everyday use, *inspire* means to be motivated or set afire by an influence, often toward a higher purpose from God or a cultivated model. Many of the authors of this volume fittingly seem inspired by their exemplars. The language they use to characterize the exemplars is positive and admiring throughout—surely warranted by the lives of those whom they studied.

We therefore believe the authors hope, without explicitly stating so, that readers too will be inspired by the exemplars they have so carefully identified and characterized. Indeed, one benefit of the extensive use of interview excerpts and careful descriptions used in all the chapters is to facilitate our appreciation of the exemplars' experiences, including their successful struggles to gain ethical ascendance. In other words, the study of exemplars and the presentation of thick descriptions of their lives, coupled with their stories of movement toward their ideals, not only satisfies intellectual curiosity about the roots of moral and spiritual excellence, but can also motivate and deepen our pursuit of ethical life. We are grateful to the authors of the chapters in this volume. We likewise express our gratitude to

NEW DIRECTIONS FOR CHILD AND ADOLESCENT DEVELOPMENT • DOI: 10.1002/cad

the exemplars who shared their time with the researchers and contributed to this most exciting project.

References

Cattell, J. M. (1903). A statistical study of eminent men. *Popular Science Monthly, LXII*, 359–377. Retrieved from http://psycnet.apa.org/psycinfo/1903-10130-005

Colby, A., & Damon, W. (1992). *Some do care: Contemporary lives of moral commitment*. New York, NY: The Free Press.

Donald, D. H. (1987). *Look homeward: A life of Thomas Wolfe*. New York, NY: Little, Brown.

Hart, D., Atkins, R., Fegley, S., Robins, R. W., & Tracy, J. L. (2003). Personality and development in childhood: A person-centered approach. *Monographs of the Society for Research in Child Development, 68*(1), 1–122. Retrieved from http://www.jstor.org/stable/10.2307/1166223

Hart, D., & Sulik, M. (in press). The social construction of volunteering. In L. Padilla-Walker & G. Carlo (Eds.), *The complexities of raising prosocial children*. New York, NY: Oxford University Press.

Hart, T. (1998). Inspiration: Exploring the experience and its meaning. *Journal of Humanistic Psychology, 38*(3), 7–35.

Howe, M. L., & Courage, M. L. (1997). The emergence and early development of autobiographical memory. *Psychological Review, 104*(3), 499–523.

Lewis, R. W. B. (1991). *The Jameses: A family narrative*. New York, NY: Farrar, Straus & Giroux.

Michel, J. B., Shen, Y. K., Aiden, A. P., Veres, A., Gray, M. K., Pickett, J. P., ... Aiden, E. L. (2011). Quantitative analysis of culture using millions of digitized books. *Science, 331*(6014), 176–182. Retrieved from http://www.sciencemag.org/content/331/6014/176

Ross, M. (1989). Relation of implicit theories to the construction of personal histories. *Psychological Review, 96*(2), 341–357.

Taylor, C. (1993). Modernity and the rise of the public sphere. *The Tanner Lectures on Human Values, 14*, 203–260.

Terman, L. M. (1926). *Genetic studies of genius. Vol. 1, Mental and physical traits of a thousand gifted children*. Stanford, CA: Stanford University Press.

Wolf, S. (1982). Moral saints. *The Journal of Philosophy, LXXIX*(8), 419–439.

DANIEL A. HART *is a professor of psychology and childhood studies at Rutgers University.*

THERESA MURZYN *is a doctoral student in childhood studies at Rutgers University–Camden.*

LISA ARCHIBALD *has taught 9th and 11th grade English in Philadelphia with Teach for America, and now researches effective ways to empower teachers and students to generate meaningful change in urban public schools and their communities.*

Index

OTHER TITLES AVAILABLE IN THE
NEW DIRECTIONS FOR CHILD AND ADOLESCENT DEVELOPMENT SERIES
Lene Arnett Jensen and Reed W. Larson, Editors-in-Chief
William Damon, Founding Editor-in-Chief

For a complete list of back issues, please visit www.josseybass.com/go/ndcad

NEW DIRECTIONS FOR CHILD AND ADOLESCENT DEVELOPMENT
ORDER FORM SUBSCRIPTION AND SINGLE ISSUES

DISCOUNTED BACK ISSUES:

Use this form to receive 20% off all back issues of *New Directions for Child and Adolescent Development*. All single issues priced at **$23.20** (normally $29.00)

TITLE	ISSUE NO.	ISBN
_____	_____	_____
_____	_____	_____

Call 888-378-2537 or see mailing instructions below. When calling, mention the promotional code JBNND to receive your discount. For a complete list of issues, please visit www.josseybass.com/go/ndcad

SUBSCRIPTIONS: (1 YEAR, 4 ISSUES)

☐ New Order   ☐ Renewal

U.S.	☐ Individual: $89	☐ Institutional: $388
CANADA/MEXICO	☐ Individual: $89	☐ Institutional: $428
ALL OTHERS	☐ Individual: $113	☐ Institutional: $462

Call 888-378-2537 or see mailing and pricing instructions below.
Online subscriptions are available at www.onlinelibrary.wiley.com

ORDER TOTALS:

Issue / Subscription Amount: $ _____

Shipping Amount: $ _____
(for single issues only – subscription prices include shipping)

Total Amount: $ _____

SHIPPING CHARGES:

First Item	$6.00
Each Add'l Item	$2.00

(No sales tax for U.S. subscriptions. Canadian residents, add GST for subscription orders. Individual rate subscriptions must be paid by personal check or credit card. Individual rate subscriptions may not be resold as library copies.)

BILLING & SHIPPING INFORMATION:

☐ **PAYMENT ENCLOSED:** *(U.S. check or money order only. All payments must be in U.S. dollars.)*

☐ **CREDIT CARD:** ☐ VISA ☐ MC ☐ AMEX

Card number _____ Exp. Date_____

Card Holder Name_____ Card Issue #_____

Signature _____ Day Phone_____

☐ **BILL ME:** *(U.S. institutional orders only. Purchase order required.)*

Purchase order # _____
Federal Tax ID 13559302 • GST 89102-8052

Name_____

Address_____

Phone_____ E-mail_____

Copy or detach page and send to: **John Wiley & Sons, One Montgomery Street, Suite 1200, San Francisco, CA 94104-4594**

Order Form can also be faxed to: **888-481-2665**

PROMO JBNND

Statement of Ownership

Statement of Ownership, Management, and Circulation (required by 39 U.S.C. 3685), filed on OCTOBER 1, 2013 for NEW DIRECTIONS FOR CHILD AND ADOLESCENT DEVELOPMENT (Publication No. 1520-3247), published Quarterly for an annual subscription price of $89 at Wiley Subscription Services, Inc., at Jossey-Bass, One Montgomery St., Suite 1200, San Francisco, CA 94104-4594.

The names and complete mailing addresses of the Publisher, Editor, and Managing Editor are: Publisher, Wiley Subscription Services, Inc., A Wiley Company at San Francisco, One Montgomery St., Suite 1200, San Francisco, CA 94104-4594; Editor, Co-Editor, Lene Arnett Jensen, Clark University, Dept. of Psychology, 950 Main Street, Worcester, MA 01610; Managing Editor, Co-Editor Reed Larson, Univ. of Illinois, dept. of Human Community Dev, 904 W. Nevada St., Urbana, IL 61801. Contact Person: Joe Schuman; Telephone: 415-782-3232.

NEW DIRECTIONS FOR CHILD AND ADOLESCENT DEVELOPMENT is a publication owned by Wiley Subscription Services, Inc., 111 River St., Hoboken, NJ 07030. The known bondholders, mortgages, and other security holders owning or holding 1% or more of total amount of bonds, mortgages, or other securities are (see list):

	Average No. Copies Each Issue During Preceding 12 Months	No. Copies of Single Issue Published Nearest To Filing Date (Summer 2013)
15a. Total number of copies (net press run)	570	378
15b. Legitimate paid and/or requested distribution (by mail and outside mail)		
15b(1). Individual paid/requested mail subscriptions stated on PS form 3541 (include direct written request from recipient, telemarketing, and Internet requests from recipient, paid subscriptions including nominal rate subscriptions, advertiser's proof copies, and exchange copies)	88	68
15b(2). Copies requested by employers for distribution to employees by name or position, stated on PS form 3541	0	0
15b(3). Sales through dealers and carriers, street vendors, counter sales, and other paid or requested distribution outside USPS	0	0
15b(4). Requested copies distributed by other mail classes through USPS	0	0
15c. Total paid and/or requested circulation (sum of 15b(1), (2), (3), and (4))	88	68
15d. Nonrequested distribution (by mail and outside mail)		
15d(1). Outside county nonrequested copies stated on PS form 3541	42	42
15d(2). In-county nonrequested copies stated on PS form 3541	0	0
15d(3). Nonrequested copies distributed through the USPS by other classes of mail	0	0
15d(4). Nonrequested copies distributed outside the mail	0	0
15e. Total nonrequested distribution (sum of 15d(1), (2), (3), and (4))	42	42
15f. Total distribution (sum of 15c and 15e)	130	110
15g. Copies not distributed	440	268
15h. Total (sum of 15f and 15g)	570	378
15i. Percent paid and/or requested circulation (15c divided by 15f times 100)	68%	61.8%

I certify that all information furnished on this form is true and complete. I understand that anyone who furnishes false or misleading information on this form or who omits material or information requested on this form may be subject to criminal sanctions (including fines and imprisonment) and/or civil sanctions (including civil penalties).

Statement of Ownership will be printed in the Winter 2013 issue of this publication.

(signed) Susan E. Lewis, VP & Publisher-Periodicals